Pottery

By Glen Pownall

ALLISON & BUSBY, *London*

Acknowledgements

Page 7 Lamp base and lidded pot *(D. Carson–Parker)*
Page 9 Plate and teapot *(Doreen Blumhardt)*
Page 13 Tall blue vases*(Graeme Storm)*
Page 43 Sculptured figures *(Muriel Moody)*
Page 53 Mosaic panel *(J. L. Stewart)*
Page 63 Maori head *(Lorna Ellis)*

All photographs supplied by Alan Seaton and Richard Silcock

SBN 85031 092 X

First published in Great Britain in 1973 by
Allison and Busby Limited
6a Noel Street, London WIV 3RB

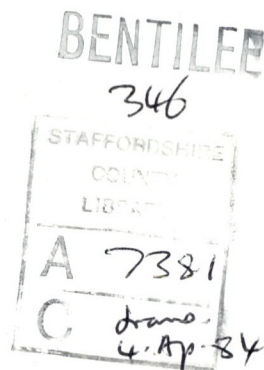

Printed in Taiwan

Contents

Pottery and you

Clay, the potter and pottery form a highly personal and entirely creative relationship. The plastic nature of clay and its ability to yield to the creative guidance of the craftsman makes the art of pottery one of the great crafts.

Pottery need not be an expensive hobby. It is true that a properly "set-up" studio, complete with ball mills, throwing wheel, pug mill and an elaborate kiln or two, requires the outlay of considerable capital. However, excellent pottery was made hundreds of centuries before there were any electrically driven machines or gas fired kilns available and if you have the will you can be a potter with the outlay of only a few dollars.

This book gives in the most practical way possible, details of how to get started in pottery and turn your leisure into creative leisure and, with some experience, your spare time into money.

Yes! That is correct. There is a world-wide shortage of hand-made individual pottery pieces and anybody who can create acceptable pottery has no difficulty selling it at quite astonishing values at times.

This book has been written with both the beginner and the moderately experienced potter in mind. The overall theme is strictly do-it-yourself and emphasis has been placed on obtaining, processing and using materials which are obtained in the same way as the primitive potters gained their materials. It is for this reason that this book will have value, even to those who have perfected their own technique and are no longer in the need of detailed instruction, but are attracted towards developing local materials in order to advance their own individual style and finishes.

The beginner will find that he or she will be guided by detailed instructions on how to begin to enjoy a great craft, with little outlay of money. From time to time, proprietary materials are given consideration. This is in deference to those who lack either the opportunity or inclination to gather their own materials.

CHAPTER ONE

From time to time throughout this book, reference will be made to the term "primitive". This reference is used to denote that inclination by many leading potters to use the materials of the hills and fields, natural materials which they work up and develop in order to produce articles that bear the stamp of their own artistry. Pottery, made from clay, glazed with pulverized rock is a hand-craft which is as far removed from the automated factories of this age as it is possible to get. This basic mode of "primitive" pottery is one of the great appeals of pottery and one that is practically unmatched by any other craft.

Working with clay

CLAY AND ITS PREPARATION

Where to find clay

Clay is one of the commonest earth substances, usually found as substrata in fields and meadows, covered with a layer of soil and plants. Farmers and country folk in general are a rich source of information on the whereabouts of clay beds and are usually prepared to grant permission to allow digging to take place on their property. Once a clay bed has been located the top soil should be cleared well back from the edge of where digging will take place. The hole should be far enough into the clay stratum to be free of stones and in particular humus (the decayed plant material so beloved of gardeners).

Considerable experience is needed to tell by looking whether any particular clay is suited to your requirements. However, if a firm, rather greasy, homogeneous clay is found, free from sand and discoloration, it is likely to be suitable for pottery making and in any case it can be tested. The usual clay found will be one of the many shades of yellow from brown through to buff, but all colours can be found – red, blue, white, even green clays do occur and each will 'fire out' a different colour, mostly, very different from its original colour. It is probably a good idea to treat a number of samples at one time and selections of clays from a number of localities will greatly increase the chances of finding a clay suited to a particular need.

Preparing Clay

There are a number of ways of bringing raw clay to a state of 'workability'. The real 'primitive' will find appeal in the following method:

(1) Clear back the top soil, well down into the clay in a circle at least 6 feet in diameter.
(2) Chip out the clay until a saucer shaped depression, say two feet deep in the centre is left, filled with the clay chips which are not removed from the hole. Incidentally, the fact that the clay comes away in chips is a fair indication of a reasonable pottery clay.
(3) Fill the depression with water, stirring and chopping the chips.
(4) Leave for several hours.
(5) Knead with bare feet, feeling for hard lumps with the toes and using

the weight of the body to break the whole mass (should we say 'mess'?) down to a putty-like consistency.

(6) Properly prepared the clay can be rolled into large sausage-like rolls and placed in damp cloths or plastic bags for transporting.

If the clay tends to be sandy or contain other impurities; if water is not available on the site of the digging or if the potter is averse to feeling wet clay oozing between toes, a more conventional method of clay preparation is adopted as follows:

(a) Cut the clay into rough blocks for transporting.

(b) Spread out the clay in small pieces in the sun or other dry place and leave to get completely dry. (Tough, leathery, partly wet clay is very difficult to render plastic as in this condition it will not readily 'take up' water).

(c) When fully dry, crush and hammer the clay until it will pass through a coarse sieve of about ¼ inch mesh. (It is not essential to carry out the operation of sifting, but it is extremely convenient.) Discard any larger lumps which will not readily break up. Do not attempt economies with clay. It is better to discard a high percentage that may be unsuitable than to spoil a complete batch.

(d) Three quarters fill a bucket or pail with the fine clay lumps and cover completely with water. The clay should take up the water immediately and this is hastened with stirring. It is at this point the temperament of a true potter comes uppermost. If by natural inclination you plunge your arm to the bottom and stir the mass with your fingers, you are a potter by inclination and well on the way to becoming a potter in fact.

(e) Leave the mixture for an hour or so, stirring occasionally until a thin, smooth 'slip' results. This slip should pour easily through a window-screen size mesh (technically a 20 mesh sieve).

(f) Leave the sifted slip overnight and pour off the more or less clear water from the top of the bucket.

(g) Pour the remainder onto a plaster bat. (See Appendix A for the making of plaster bats or slabs.) The plaster quickly absorbs the excess moisture and after a period, the clay stiffens and curls back from the plaster. The clay can then be picked up and stored in plastic bags for later use.

Two semi-technical terms are used by some potters to describe clay:

(i) *Short Clay*, which is too sandy and inclined to crumble when being worked.

(ii) *Fat Clay*, which is jelly-like and appears to be highly plastic. While appearing to be suitable for working, fat clay will slump and the shape worked into it, will be lost.

Short clay and fat clay have mutually contrasting properties and are the starting points from which clay of special composition can be obtained.

Storing Clay

Plastic clay, ready for final processing before working should not be allowed to dry out. Plastic bags with the end sealed by means of a rubber band do very well and allow workable quantities of clay to be stored. Larger quantities can be held in a crockery crock with a tight fitting lid, while very large amounts can be held in non-corrosive metal (copper, zinc or aluminium) or plastic lined boxes with airtight lids.

Testing Clay

The suitability of clay for pottery depends largely on its' 'firing out' qualities. If a clay produces acceptable pottery when fired under the particular circumstance of an individual potter, then it is a good pottery clay. From this it obviously follows that the true test of a clay is to fire an object made from that clay and test it by 'doing'. However, this course is not always convenient and the following procedure can be adopted to give a fair indication of the satisfactory nature of a given clay:

(1) Take a lump of clay the approximate size of a fist.

(2) Roll a small piece into a ball and drop it on a hard surface. If the ball splits or crumples, either the clay is not good pottery clay, or the preparation has been incomplete.

(3) Roll a slab about $\frac{1}{2}$ inch in thickness and, with a sharp knife, cut a block about 2 inches wide and $8\frac{1}{2}$ or 9 inches long. Put two marks on the clay exactly 8 inches apart and set the block aside to dry in an airy, not too warm, but dry situation. Examine when perfectly dry. If the block shows no sign of cracking or crumbling and if the distance between the marks is $7\frac{1}{2}$ inches or more, the clay will probably be quite satisfactory.

The above tests are only an indication that the clay is worth a trial but tell little of the way it will behave in the actual kiln to be used. For instance, the kiln may not be capable of reaching the temperature needed to fuse a given clay and the only test of this is to try the clay under firing conditions.

Buying Clay

Prepared clay may be bought from a number of sources: brick works, pottery manufacturers (sometimes) and craft and hobby shops. If prepared clay is purchased it will be in a similar condition to the clay which has been prepared in accordance with the discussion above and can be immediately put into storage.

Clay can be bought in bulk quantities from a hundred weight to quantities of a ton or more, but is usually obtainable, less economically, in smaller quantities. Dry powdered clay is sometimes supplied and it should be prepared in accordance with the supplier's instructions.

While circumstances may make it essential to buy prepared clay, there is no doubt that clay so obtained lacks an intimate connection with the potter, an intimacy which is really a great part of the feeling for clay which makes a great potter. On the more practical side is the unconscious urge to conserve a material which has been purchased and this detracts from the feeling of expansiveness which adds to the freedom of expression leading to outstanding work.

Studio or Work Place

This is where real work begins, some of it requiring a good deal of effort. Pottery is not a craft which can be carried out in a corner of the lounge. Inside the home, the kitchen is likely to be as close as one can get to a suitable work room and can be entirely satisfactory provided:

(a) A heavy table or ample size strong bench can be used as a work place.

(b) Any clay falling on the floor can be cleanly and rapidly removed so no fear of 'tracking' clay into other rooms exists.

(c) Storage is available for tools, equipment, clay and partly finished work.

An airy, well lighted shed, basement or enclosed porch can be used as an ideal studio. The following comments on the suitability of a room or other premises for use as a pottery studio are pertinent:

(1) Ample space is necessary. Quite a lot of equipment of one sort or another needs to be stored and it is nigh on impossible to do good work in cramped, cluttered surroundings.

(2) Good lighting is a must. This need not necessarily be daylight. In fact ample, well dispersed, non-glaring artificial light is far better than poor daylight filtered through trees, reflected off walls and carrying moving shadows and a large change in intensity as the sun moves.

(3) Pottery work requires good ventilation at an even temperature while drying out. There must be, of necessity, large quantities of water vapour released while pottery pieces dry out and if trapped inside, this moisture will rust tools, cause mould growth and generally prove unpleasant.

(4) Even temperature. If the temperature drops below freezing point, partly finished pieces will be ruined. Besides, it is impossible to freeze in the winter, stew in the summer, and still work well. This requirement rejects

9

Figure 1.1

turnbuckle for
tightening wire

wood 18"×3"×1"
screwed to rear
of box

piano wire or stainless
steel wire about
18 s.w.g

plaster
of Paris

screw

wooden box 15"×15"×6"

wedging board

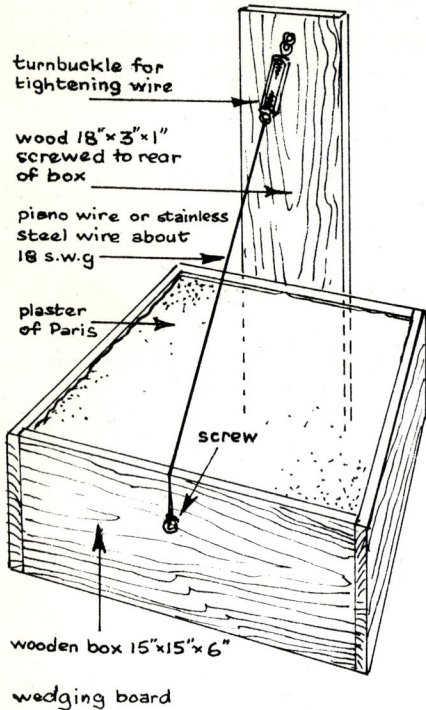

unlined sheds and the like. If it is impossible to find suitable enclosed premises the alternative is to work outdoors when the weather is suitable. Outdoor work is pleasant and some of the world's leading potters seize every opportunity of doing as much of their creative work outdoors as is practical.

(5) The premises must be suited to the use of wet objects and at times largish quantities of water. There is no need for a pottery studio to ever become awash but accidents will happen and this possibility must be taken into account.

Final preparation of clay

Clay taken out of storage requires further working before it can be used for modelling, throwing or other pottery techniques.

Certain equipment is needed as follows:

(1) *A wedging board:* Figure 1.1 shows a wedging board and the way it is made. A wedging board essentially consists of a thick Plaster of Paris base over which is a fine, high tensile strength wire (which can be purchased at hardware merchants), held diagonally in tension and used for cutting plastic clay. A long bladed knife can substitute for the wire and any flat surface can be used for wedging, but the small cost and lack of difficulty in making a wedging board as shown is more than recovered in the convenience of carrying out the tiring chore of hand-wedging.

(2) *A scraper:* A plastic pot scraper does an excellent job of lifting the clay that adheres to the surface of the wedging board.

(3) A plastic sponge and a few damp cloths.

The process of wedging is essential to condition the clay by removing air bubbles and making it uniform in texture. If the clay is too dry, extra moisture, squeezed on from the wet sponge can be thoroughly incorporated during wedging. If the clay is too wet, wedging will remove the required amount of moisture, especially if use is made of the type of wedging board described above. The plaster base of the wedging board will extract moisture quickly from the clay.

To carry out the wedging process, proceed as follows:

(a) Take a lump of clay of a size convenient to one's physical capabilities in two hands and pass it over the wire so that it is cut in half.

(b) Throw one half on the board and then throw the other half on top to form one lump. Slam the lumps together with some force.

(c) Repeat the process at least twenty times to ensure that there are no cavities showing on the cut face of the last cut. The colour and texture should appear completely uniform with no stripes or shading and of an even content before the wedging process is finished.

And that brings the clay to a state where reasonably effective results can be expected in the making of pottery pieces.

Perhaps the clay will have changed very little in the processing but the potter will have grown in his feelings toward the clay upon which he now can impress his creativity.

CHAPTER TWO

From clay to pots

The potter's wheel has come to be the almost universal symbol of the potter's art. A particular creative satisfaction comes from the flow of plastic clay, moving beneath one's hands on a potter's wheel. The clay flows from a lump of lifeless mud, in one continuous movement, to become a shape in which is frozen the personal inner urges of creativity. No other medium expresses this sense of frozen movement, caught for all time at an instant of change. This is the basis of the visual and tactile stimulation arising from 'throwing' pots on a potter's wheel.

Despite the unique satisfaction inherent in 'throwing' pots, the fluidity of prepared clay gives scope for an infinity of expressions and among the real masterpieces of pottery are many which have not originated on a potter's wheel. It is with these alternative techniques that primitive potters can gain a great deal of satisfaction and understanding of clay, later moving to the wheel if the need arises.

Thumbed pots

The ancient Japanese revered tea bowls made entirely by hand through the manipulation of thumb and fingers. This surely is the most basic of all pottery processes, the tools, eight fingers and two thumbs; the material, very plastic clay that will move readily with no tendency to crack or crumble when squeezed and handled. The instructions are simplicity itself:

Take a ball of clay, work it well between the hands, roll it between the palms until it flows and lives. Roll into a ball and make a hole in the centre with a thumb; pinch the walls and base to an even thickness with fingers and thumbs, not hesitating to collapse an indifferent result and begin again.

The shape becomes what your imagination dictates, the finish what your patience and skill allows. When finished to your satisfaction, place on a clean board in an airy, even temperature shelf or cupboard and leave in preparation for firing as discussed in Chapter 7. Thumbed pots, simple in conception, easy to achieve, with each finished piece unique to its maker, are the natural starting point of creative pottery.

There are those teachers who would always start children and beginners in the art of pottery on the technique of 'thumbing' and this must be recognised as a most sympathetic beginning point. It is here that the intimacy between clay and potter begins to become apparent. The intimacy which marks the true artists; the feeling as to the limits that the living clay will allow; the way to recognise and check manipulations which are outside the nature of clay to withstand; these are learned better without artificial tools using only the control of human hands.

Many eminent contemporary potters beginning with 'thumbing' have never felt the urge to change from this technique. Textures and patterns may be impressed into the surface finish; shapes can be as varied as the imagination of the artist; clay shapes, pellets, coils, and tablets applied to the surface; different coloured clays incorporated and in fact all the multifarious operations of pottery decorations can be extended to thumbed work.

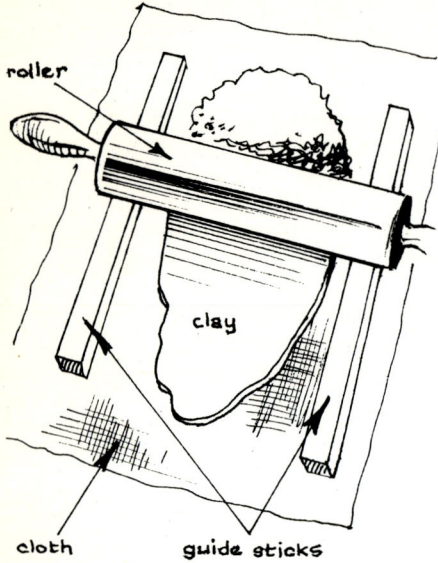

Figure 2.1

roller

clay

cloth

guide sticks

Figure 2.2

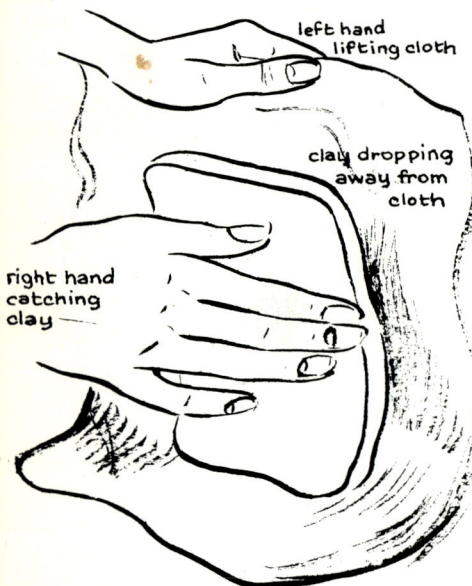

left hand
lifting cloth

clay dropping
away from
cloth

right hand
catching
clay

Tools and machinery have their own appeal and a natural impatience can result in a craftsman neglecting to fully extend the methods of hand manipulation of clay. This is probably a mistake for surely it is the living mode of clay that is to be cultivated for true artistry. Tools, of any sort, are simply time-savers, and the ultimate in tool using is mass production where the greatest designs become contemptuous through repetition. Even where quantity production is the aim it is good advice to suggest that from time to time the craftsman renews his intimate acquaintance with living clay by a hand manipulative technique such as 'thumbing'.

Slab pottery

Slab pottery should perhaps be regarded as an extension of thumbed techniques insofar as tool using methods are used to save time and to some extent standardize the material to be worked. Slab pottery is the use of flat, cut slabs of clay to produce pottery articles of various shapes.

To make the clay slabs of uniform thickness the following equipment is needed:

(1) Rolling pin or parallel sided bottle.
(2) A piece of canvas, burlap or coarse calico.

The procedure for 'slabbing' is simple:
(a) The cloth is dampened to prevent taking moisture from the clay and laid on a flat, firm table or bench.
(b) Two sticks of suitable, identical thickness are laid parallel on the cloth at the maximum distance spanned by the rolling pin. See *Figure 2.1*.
(c) Flatten a ball of worked clay between the palms to a thickness somewhat greater than the thickness of the sticks and place on the cloth.
(d) With a wet roller, roll once each way from the middle. Rolling several times will cause the clay to stick to the cloth.
(e) Lift the cloth and drop the clay slab into your free hand after each complete pass with the roller. This operation is shown in *Figure 2.2*.
(f) Continue until the clay slab has reached the required thickness.

If insufficient clay has been taken in the first place, add extra clay only by moulding the old and new by hand and not by attempting to consolidate the two masses by rolling. If a square or round slab is required, the the starting point is a flattened ball of clay. If an oval or oblong shape is needed, start with a flattened fat sausage-like mass of clay.

Thickness of slabs

For small slabware the thickness of the clay can be about a $\frac{1}{4}$ of an inch or a little less. Larger pots will require thicker walls and it may be necessary to support the walls until the clay becomes partly dry (reaches the leather stage the experienced potter will say).

Grog

Clay when completely dry contains chemically combined water which must be released during the firing. A solid lump of clay, an inch or more in thickness, will almost certainly break when fired through lack of openings to let this water vapour escape. One way to avoid such breakages is to keep all walls and bases less than $\frac{1}{2}$ an in inch in thickness. This can be achieved by judicious hollowing of thick pieces where this is practical.

Another way, which has more universal application, is to combine 'grog' with the clay before working. Grog is clay which has been fired, ground and screened. Grog can be obtained ready for use from shops supplying the needs of potters but the beginner, alas, has an all too plentiful supply of potential grog available from projects that have failed.

To make grog, break up unglazed fired clay. This can be done in a deep heavy box, pounding the grog with a square-ended steel bar. A broken automobile rear axle is ideal for this. The most useful grade of grog is one that will go through a sieve with a mesh of 30 meshes to the inch but not fine enough to go through a 60 mesh sieve.

For most purposes, one handful of grog will be mixed with two handfuls

12

of clay. The grog should be soaked in water and then left to drain for a few minutes before mixing with the clay. The use of sufficient grog will obviate the need to hollow pottery and it will tend to prevent warping. Obviously grog on the surface of clay will show in the finished work and while in some cases this will not be a disadvantage in general it should be avoided. In the case of slabware, the grog for heavy slabs can be added on top after the rolling process, and then rolled part-way through the clay.

Figure 2.3

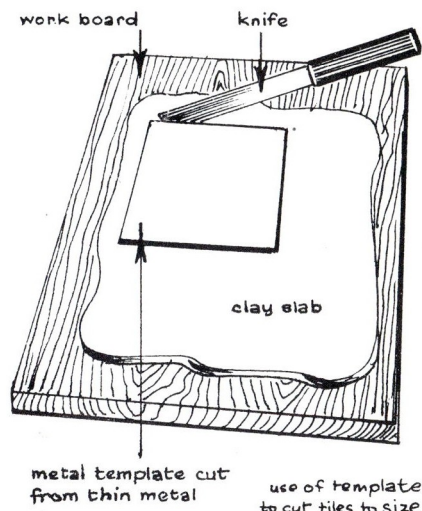

work board   knife

clay slab

metal template cut
from thin metal

use of template
to cut tiles to size

Tile making

Ceramic or pottery tiles have a wide appeal and numerous useful applications. Very small tiles can be used in mosaic work where they are called tesserae and cemented to form patterns on the surface of a variety of objects.

Individual hand decorated tiles fetch very high prices and are well worthwhile making. Tiles are made as follows:

(a) A template (*Figure 2.3*) is cut from metal and used as a guide for cutting the tile from the clay slab. Allowance for shrinking of the clay during drying to the leather stage and then further shrinking during firing must be allowed in the template. Clays vary in the amount they shrink. The only satisfactory way to judge the size to cut a template is to make a couple of test tiles and fire them. However, for most uses, the tiles need not be any particular size as long as they all end up the same size, so if a template is made in the form of a square with sides 4⅞ inches long, the chances are that the finished tile will not depart greatly from the standard size of a commercial ceramic tile.

(b) Heavily grogged clay is really needed for tile making. Certainly this is so for beginners and those not experienced in firing flat pottery pieces. The thickness of the tile can be around ⅜ inch but can be made much thinner.

(c) The skill in tile making is ensuring that the tile neither warps nor becomes mis-shapen. Careful drying between Plaster of Paris slabs will go far to ensure that tiles will at least reach the leather stage without damage. A tall sandwich of alternate tiles and smooth surfaced plaster bats is made as shown in *Figure 2.4*. The making of plaster bats is discussed in Appendix A.

(d) The decoration of tiles is given a separate section in Chapter 5 to which reference should be made. Chapter 7 deals with the technique of firing.

Structural strength of clay

True art springs spontaneously from the nature of the material one is handling. So it is with clay work. Patience and care cannot create an artwork from a piece of tortured clay. Grotesqueries perhaps, monstrosities often, mis-shapes usually result if clay is deformed and expected to maintain a position that is contrary to the nature of clay.

The most obvious fact about a plastic clay slab is the lack of structural strength. A clay slab in working condition will not support its own weight. Stood on edge it will buckle and collapse. Sharp square edges will be subject to stress in the firing which will inevitably weaken the piece if it does not crack it right then. And so it goes. At the risk of stressing the self-evident, let us say once again that great potters are made from the feeling of oneness that potter has with the clay with which he works. Hence the nature of clay while it is wet; the direction in which it shrinks, while drying to the leather stage; the way it behaves while being tooled (discussed in Chapter 5); and the way the high temperature stresses are distributed throughout the body while firing are the facts of clay and the guide lines, within which a potter must work.

Clay shapes

Flat clay slabs can be made self-supporting if made in girder shapes. A

Figure 2.4

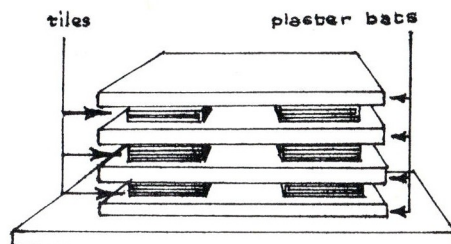

tiles   plaster bats

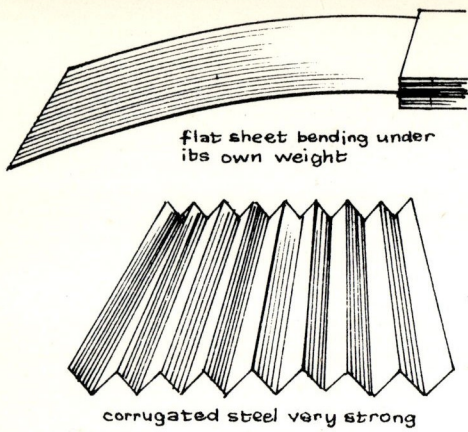

flat sheet bending under its own weight

corrugated steel very strong

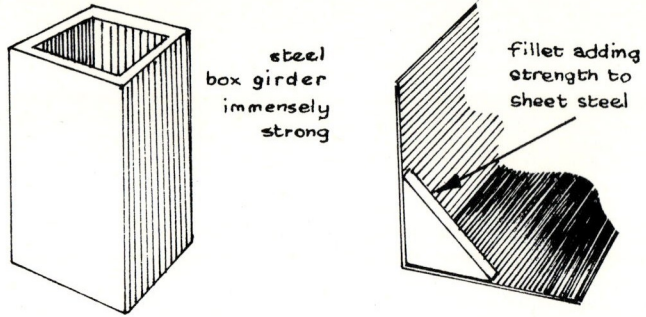

Figure 2.5

steel box girder immensely strong

fillet adding strength to sheet steel

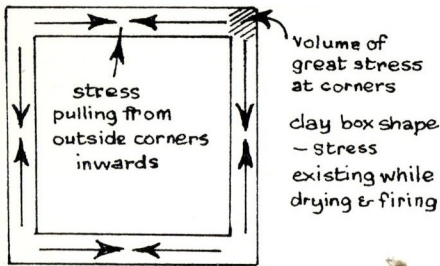

stress pulling from outside corners inwards

Volume of great stress at corners

clay box shape – stress existing while drying & firing

Figure 2.6

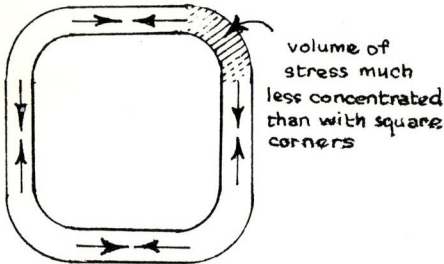

volume of stress much less concentrated than with square corners

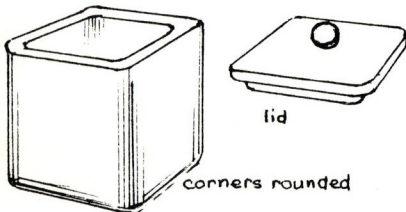

lid

corners rounded

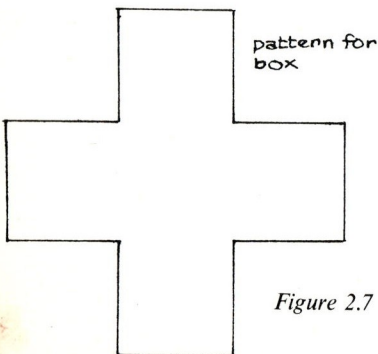

pattern for box

Figure 2.7

sheet of steel has little strength – it will wave and flex when lifted by one edge. However, bend it into a box shape, form right angle corrugations in it or add fillets and reinforcing pieces to it and with all these modifications it gains in structural strength, becoming immensely strong. *Figure 2.5.*

Clay slabs have much in common with simple steel sheets and can be made self-supporting in a similar way. However, to duplicate steel shapes without reservation is to take the risk of breakage during firing. And this for the following reason – clay turns to pottery when heated, owing to chemical and physical changes which take place in the constituents at elevated temperatures. In other words, pottery is an entirely different substance to the clay from which it comes. The inner material of the clay must re-adjust during the process and this sets up stress within the substance. Consult *Figure 2.6* where this is shown very much over-simplified. Note that rounding the corners of the box shape has decreased the distance through which the force has to operate, tending to break the corner away. At the same time, the volume of material subject to the breaking stress is greatly increased.

Figure 2.6 demonstrates a lesson which every aspiring potter must take very much to heart if disappointment is to be avoided, through pieces constantly breaking during firing.

Joining clay
Despite all the discouragement offered in the preceding paragraphs, square shapes can be made successfully and also be made to appear attractive. But the lessons offered above should be observed. The procedure is as follows:

(1) The pattern for say a box shape should be laid out to minimize the number of joins. This is shown in *Figure 2.7*. Note that the bottom and sides are cut in a cruciform shape and not as separate slabs. It would be easier to cut separate slabs for bottom and sides but the joins would be less strong if all were butt joints rather than natural bends and the finished piece would be more akin to the result of cabinet making than pottery.
(2) The pattern is marked through onto the soft clay with a narrow blunt instrument.
(3) A sharp knife working with the blade held vertically onto a cutting board is used to cut out the pattern.
(4) Eight slim clay rods about ¼ inch in diameter are rolled between palm and flat surface and of sufficient length to reach from the bottom the full height of the sides.
(5) With the cruciform shape flat on a flat surface, lift, coax might be the better term, the first two adjacent sides into place. Assist the clay to bend without cracking by bending around a thick pencil or dowel. Pinch the clay together at the point of joining to hold the two walls in place and position the remaining two walls.
(6) With wet hands, roll the clay rods to make them more plastic than the slabs and with one on the outside and one on the inside of each joint, work them well into the sides and bottom. (See *Figure 2.8*.)

16

Figure 2.8

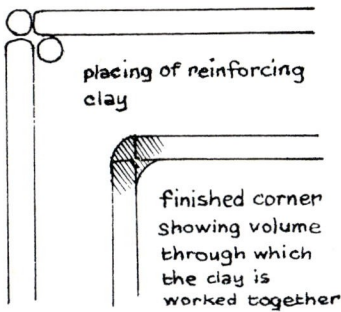

placing of reinforcing clay

finished corner showing volume through which the clay is worked together

Figure 2.9

box lid

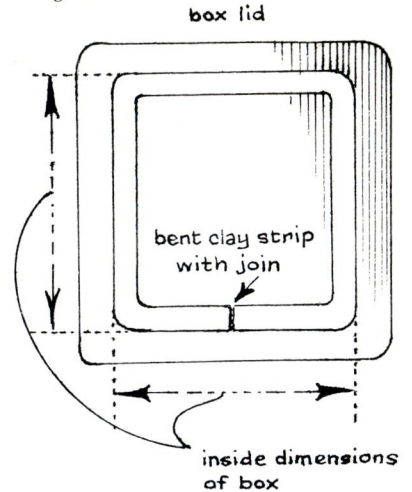

bent clay strip with join

inside dimensions of box

(7) With wet hands, work the outside of the corners until the adjacent slabs flow well into each other. Note – wet clay will stick, but unless the adjacent clay is worked to be a homogeneous whole such a join will always be a weakness in the structure. The ideal in this case is to work the extra clay from the rods and the clay from the sides so that there is no way of telling where the actual join takes place.

(8) Using a flat piece of wood or plastic as a support, straighten the sides. Round off the corners and smooth. If absolutely essential, extra clay which cannot be worked into the shape can be trimmed away with a knife. Wetting the blade will assist in making a clean cut.

(9) Small pellets of clay can be worked into the inside corners between bottom and sides. Care must be taken to ensure that there are no thin places in the joins.

(10) The lid is easily made. The slab should be larger than the box. A long strip is cut from the slab about $\frac{1}{2}$ inch wide and fitted to the lid as shown in *Figure 2.9*. Use the same technique, modified to suit, to fasten this strip to the lid as was used in making the joins in the box corners.

(11) Fit a handle to the lid of one of the types, or any other, shown in *Figure 2.10*.

(12) Put the box aside to leather. Drying to the leather stage should take place slowly and should preferably be carried out in a damp box, the construction of which is described in Appendix B.

The detailed instructions for making the box above are given as a general guide for the making of any box shape from clay slabs. A few other possible projects are given in *Figure 2.11*.

Slab sculpture

Pottery designed within the limitations of the clay has an inherent appeal, a beauty that is all its own. Modern sculpture shapes are noted for the clean lines and balance incorporated into an economy of design, giving a refreshing sense of simplicity. Pottery, or rather clay, which will eventually become pottery, lends itself very well to this simplicity and can result in most rewarding pieces.

Figure 2.12 gives some suggestions for such sculpture pieces achieved from manipulating clay slabs. For heavy work the clay must be heavily grogged using coarser grog than was discussed earlier.

Basket ware

Possibly the first mass production method ever used by man was the rather interesting process of making basket pots. The basket must be close woven and is used as a mould on which clay is packed to form a pot. The method is as follows:

(1) Take or make a cane or plastic woven basket of an interesting shape and not too large. As the clay pot is to be removed in the leather stage the basket must have a sufficiently large opening to allow the pot to be removed without difficulty.

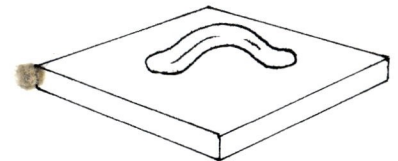

Figure 2.10

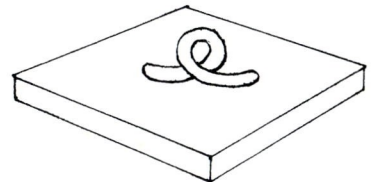

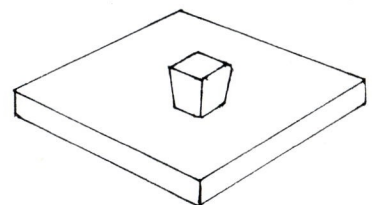

alternative handles

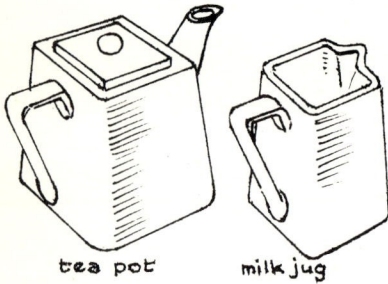

tea pot   milk jug

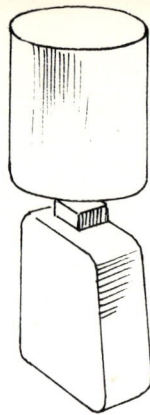 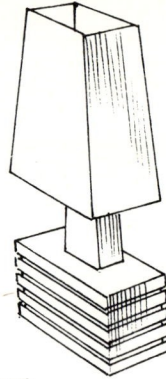

lamp bases

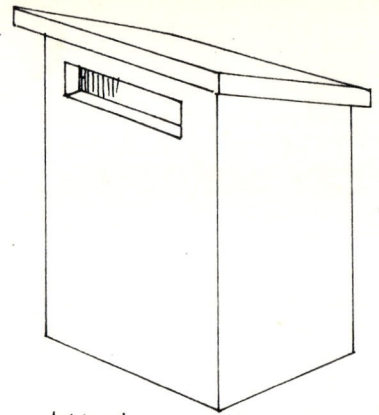

letter box

Figure 2.11

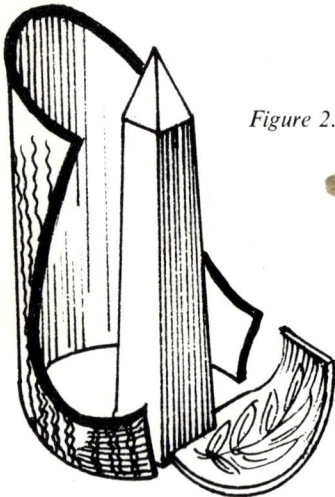

Figure 2.12

slab sculpture

(2) A natural cane basket must be well varnished or sealed with a wood sealer to render the cane reasonably impervious to moisture from the clay.

(3) Clay, rather drier than normally used, is plastered in successive layers over the inside of the basket. The clay must be well worked together without forcing the clay too far into the crevices between the weave.

(4) When the plaster is of even thickness, the basket is put in a dry, airy, cool place to slowly dry. In drying, the clay will evenly contract so that in the leather stage it can be continuously worked loose from the weave. It is then ready for firing.

Basket ware will have interesting weave patterns impressed on the surface. The rather unusual shapes and the distinctive patterns have a wide appeal and there is surely no simpler way of producing repetitive work.

A variation on this technique is to plaster either the inside or outside of a rush or other basket and then fire the work without removing the basket. The basket is fired away and this is the method used by some primitive potters to this day.

Coiled pots

A method of pottery making that is still widely practised by some eminent potters is building up the shape by using coils of clay ropes. It is a mistake to consider that coil pottery is crude or juvenile. The opposite is the case for the coil method which is, at times, the most practical way of producing a 'free form' or other sophisticated shape.

The condition of the clay for coil making is important, for not even a genius could use clay unsuited to coil making and come up with a successful piece. Therefore the essential starting point for coil work is the test of the clay, which is carried out as follows:

(1) On a piece of board (which is smooth, clean and dry), roll out a length of clay to about the diameter of and twice as long as a lead pencil.

(2) The clay must not adhere either to the hands or the board and must not have any hard lumps or other irregularities. Any grog in the clay must not be apparent.

(3) The rod of clay must not show any sign of cracking or crumbling when wound serpent-wise two or three times around the thumb.

If the clay does not satisfactorily respond to the above test it is essential to find some that does, even though it is necessary to go back to the wedging board as discussed in Chapter 1.

Clay in the correct condition can be kept that way for a fair length of time by covering loosely with a damp cloth and each length of clay as it is made should be so treated.

Clay ropes

For coil work, large quantities of clay formed into a rope-like shape are essential. There are at least two ways of doing this, the first is the one

vases

planter

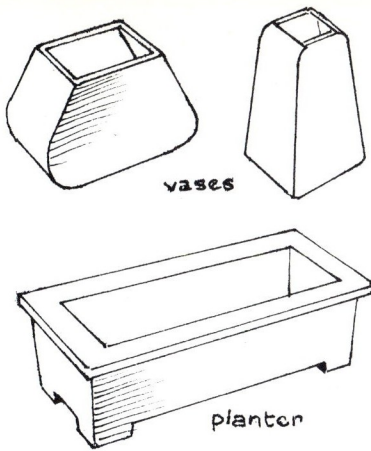

requiring least experience, but is less satisfactory in the long run. The procedure is as follows:

(1) On a large, flat, clean, smooth, damp board, start rolling out a lump of clay which had previously been squeezed into a sausage shape. Note – the board must be kept damp, not wet. This can be achieved by a pass over the surface with a heavily dampened sponge. It must be realised that keeping the board damp departs from the conditions under which the clay was tested. This is so for the reason that the test is more stringent than required and because in actual building, the clay will have more time to lose moisture and be subject to a lot more working.

(2) Use the hands with fingers outstretched, touching the clay lightly to roll into lengths. Avoid bumping the clay onto the board. The resultant 'flat' will take a lot of working out. As the clay lengthens, increase the finger pressure slightly and stroke outwards with both hands from the middle while still continuing to roll. The above may seem a complicated manoeuvre but is not difficult to acquire. (See *Figure 2.13*).

(3) In particular, see that the ends do not work thinner than the middle. Keep the fingers playing over the full length of the developing rope.

(4) If the operation goes awry, do not attempt to remedy it on the board but pick it up, reform it into a ball and start again. This is an excellent principle to adopt in clay working. If the operation does not go smoothly towards success, start again. Particularly is this principle important when extra clay has to be added.

(5) Work each length, cut off the ends if rough or elongated and store under a damp cloth.

The second, and more professional method of rope forming, is very much faster than the above method. An experienced potter will turn out length after length with amazing dexterity, almost too fast to follow. This word of encouragement is necessary, for a potter, inexperienced in this method, is liable to despair of achieving a satisfactory result on the first attempt. However, a little practice and quite suddenly one is producing length after length of highly satisfactory rope. The way to achieve such results is as follows:

(1) Take a fist size piece of clay, squeeze and slap it between the palms until it is a highly plastic pear shape.

(2) With the fingers tightly together and using the whole hand, cause the clay to extrude below the lower hand. Use both hands, from time to time reversing the clay. (See *Figure 2.14*).

(3) The rope should always hang free below the hands. If it falls back over the hand or kinks badly, start again from the ball stage.

(4) Store the finished lengths under a damp cloth. It may be that an inexperienced potter may see fit to finish the rope by using the rolling technique on the board. This is time consuming and unless practice is consistent, proficiency can never be gained in producing satisfactory ropes by the extrusion method.

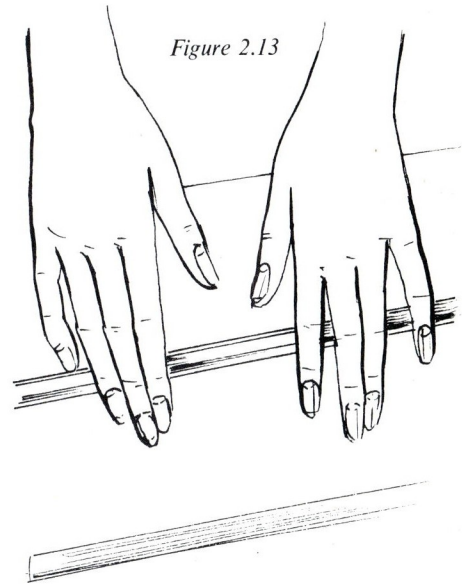

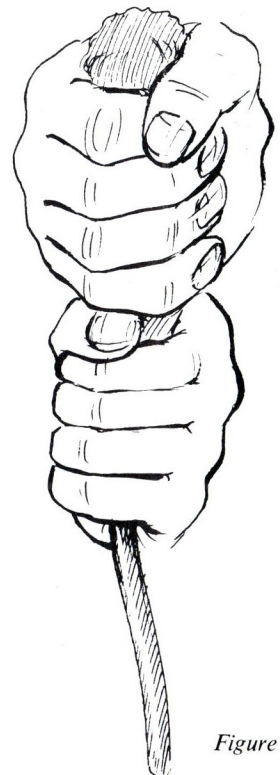

Figure 2.13

Figure 2.14

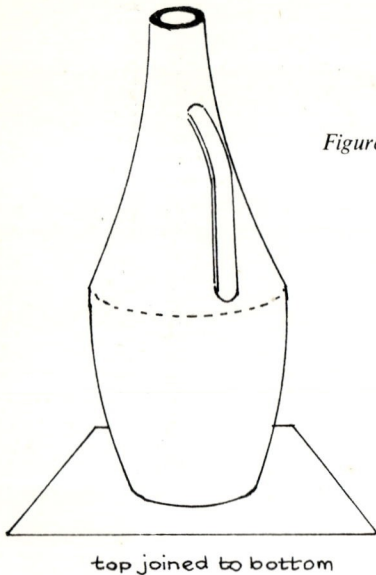

Figure 2.15

top joined to bottom

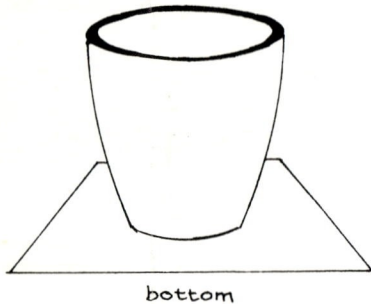

bottom

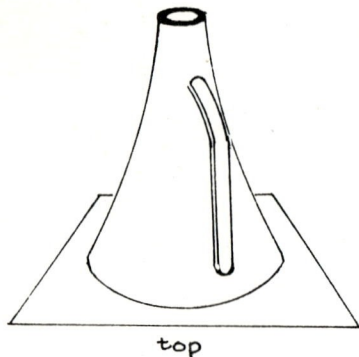

top

Clay Pulling
This is a method normally used for producing very thin ropes as used for handles, particularly on 'thrown' ware. It is mentioned here for it has a lot in common with the extrusion process, differing mainly in having the clay very wet and the stroking, pulling movement used to pull the clay from the holding hand. It is a very effective way to produce short, rather thin clay rope, but it is difficult to maintain an even thickness with long ropes such as are used in coil making.

The hands and the clay must be kept wet during the pulling operation and this may result in the finished pulled rope needing to be set aside before it can be used. Despite the inherent disadvantages of pulling clay it is a process which must be used at times and some practice in making ropes by this method will not go amiss.

Building coiled pots
Flexibility is the keynote of coiled pot making. Basically the potter has a mass of clay which is in the form of plastic clay ropes and he puts this clay together in any form that his imagination suggests. This is the real appeal of the coiled method. The only discipline is instituted by the potter himself and the inherent nature of the clay. Do the right things and quite unique objects can result; go beyond the limitations imposed by the clay and either there is a formless slumped mass of clay to go back into storage, or a fresh supply of grog if the failure occurred in the kiln.

Some potters will not consider beginning work until they have a design laid out on paper. Others, equally successful, let a piece develop as it goes together. As far as the final result the merit of either approach lies entirely in the temperament of the individual. However, there are a few general rules which must be followed to produce success, unless reliance is placed on miracles.

The making of a small bowl by the coil method is described to bring out the main points. The procedure is as follows:

(1) Roll a ball of plastic clay and flatten it to a disc of about ½ inch in thickness.
(2) For ease of working, place the disc on a round bat or even better, on a turntable.
(3) Moisten the top outer edge of the clay disc with a small brush and roughen with a small scraper. Note a list of tools is given in Chapter 6.
(4) Take a length of clay rope. Roughly measure it to be slightly longer than will fit completely around the roughened portion of the disc and break it at this point with a twisting motion.
(6) With wet fingers, work this first coil well into the base and firmly join the ends as previously discussed in slab joining.
(7) Roughen and moisten the top of the first ring and add a second ring paying particular attention to working each ring into a homogeneous whole.
(8) Repeat until four coils have been laid in place. Work, with fingers and

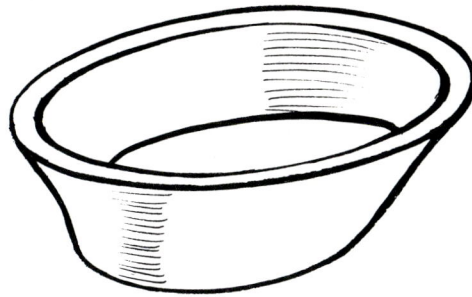

Figure 2.16

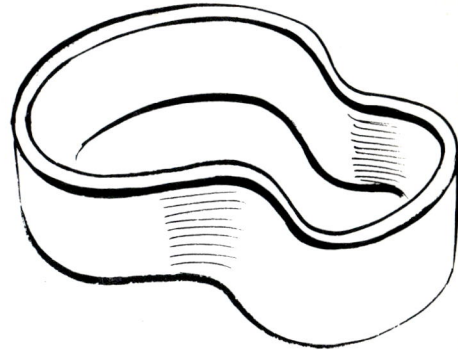

thumb around the rings, consolidating the clay and adding a flare to the pot. Speed is essential. A firm pressure should be used and care should be taken to ensure the walls are the same thickness throughout.

(9) With four rings in place, the walls may show a tendency to sag. If this happens, do not hesitate to put it to one side to harden for a time and then resume building. Remember that the top edge of the last ring must always be roughened and well moistened before the next coil is added. This is doubly important if the pot has been allowed to partially dry.

(10) Each potter tends to determine his own way of adding and working the coils into place. Do not hesitate to use tools and other equipment if it helps. The top edge can be finally trimmed with a knife. When completed, the pot can be placed to one side for drying to the leather stage.

Alternative coil work

Wide mouth pots can be more readily handled with less tendency to slump if built upside down. The first coil, which will be the rim of the pot is laid on a plaster bat. A chalked line of the shape of the rim will aid in laying down the first coil.

Large complicated shapes can be made in two pieces and carefully joined later. This technique is shown in *Figure 2.15*.

Oval and free form shapes come naturally into the field of coiled work. Some possible shapes are shown in *Figure 2.16*.

The tendency for most potters is to pass onto 'throwing' as soon as possible and then become caught up in the fascination of making pots on the wheel. This is a very natural reaction, but it has resulted in there being a dearth of pottery shapes other than those which come from throwing on a wheel and this is a loss to buyers who wish to purchase handcrafted pottery which is different. A potter who wishes to enter a market having a demand for something different could do well to consider developing coil methods into an individual style.

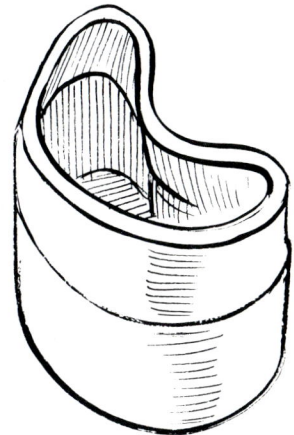

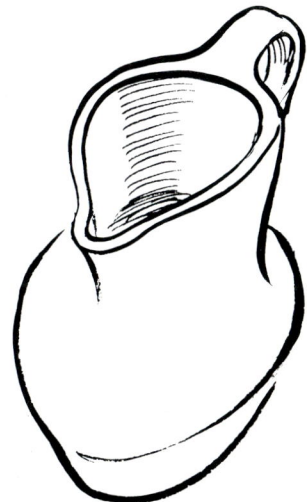

free form shapes

CHAPTER THREE

The Potter's wheel

Figure 3.1

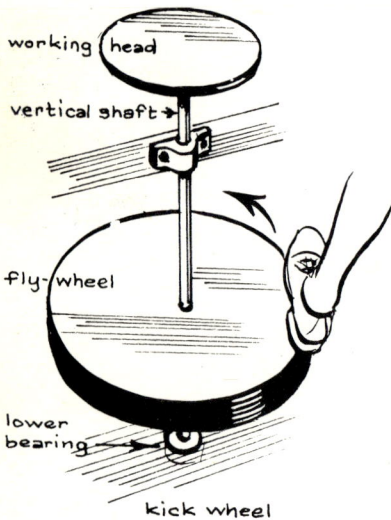

working head

vertical shaft

fly-wheel

lower bearing

kick wheel

Figure 3.2

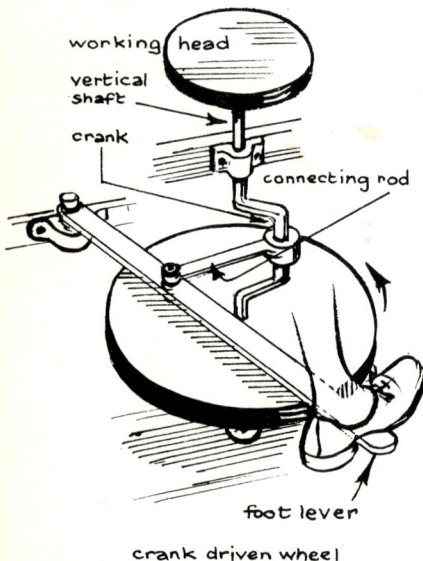

working head

vertical shaft

crank

connecting rod

foot lever

crank driven wheel

Throwing

A potter urging a mass of mud (clay) into a form of grace and elegance on a potter's wheel most truely feels that his creativity has given some touch of rare magic to the wheel. As the clay flows and lives beneath his hands, the rotation of the wheel is changed to a rhythmic sense of artistry which cannot be translated into words. No other material than clay has this capacity to obey and solidify the creative urge; no other technique than 'throwing' can give this feel of flowing movement in the creation of a thing of beauty.

The potter's wheel

With its beginnings lost in pre-history, the potter's wheel has come to us in several different forms –

The horizontal disc wheel (*Figure 3.1*) where the potter kicks a heavy horizontal fly-wheel which is rigidly connected by a vertical shaft to the working head of the wheel.

The lever and crank wheel (*Figure 3.2*). In this type of wheel the potter moves a foot operated lever backwards and forwards in a rhythmic movement which after some experience becomes co-ordinated with the movement of the hands on the clay. A crank converts the backward and forward movement to rotary motion and a vertical shaft conveys this motion to the wheel head.

The electric driven wheel which still follows the basic design of a vertical shaft with working head above but is driven by an electric motor. The motor speed may or may not be controlled by a foot operated speed controller. Many potters feel that in losing the rhythm, implicit in kicking the wheel or lever, much of the fluid movement of pottery throwing is lost. This may well be so, for there seems to be some connection between foot and hand movement when drawing a pot and this is certainly lost when electricity is used to drive the wheel. An electric potter's wheel is certainly more expensive than a kick wheel and especially is this so when a kick wheel is made by the potter himself. Against this is the fact that a table model, electrically driven wheel, is very much more compact than a kick wheel and therefore may be the only choice of a potter with a limited amount of space in which to work.

Wheel heads

A typical work head on a potter's wheel is made of metal, sometimes wood, and is a flat disc up to approximately ¾ inch in thickness though usually lighter than this. When the pot is finished, the trick is then to cut the pot free with a fine wire cutter and not cause the very plastic pot to distort or slump. This art, and it is quite an art with heavy complicated pots, is shown diagramatically in *Figure 3.3*.

An increasing number of wheels offered for sale by craft shops are fitted with what is termed a 'drop-head'. This is illustrated in *Figure 3.4*. This type of working head must be fitted with a plaster bat before throwing can be done. The big advantage of the drop-head is the ability given to lift

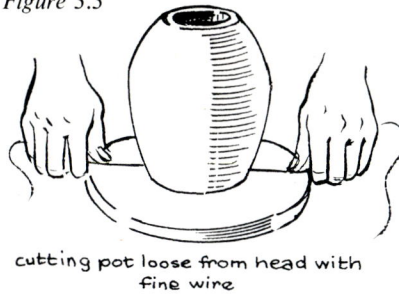

Figure 3.3

cutting pot loose from head with
fine wire

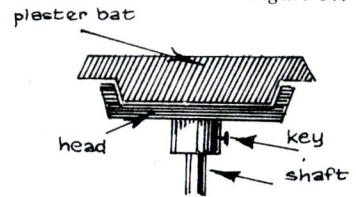

Figure 3.4

plaster bat

head   key

shaft

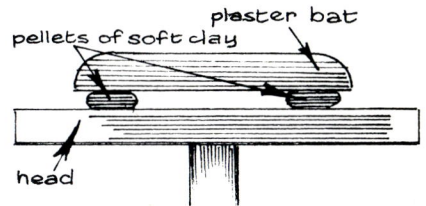

Figure 3.5

plaster bat

pellets of soft clay

head

bat and pot together away from the wheel. If necessary the head together with the pot can be replaced on the wheel and will still be found to run true. If a wheel is purchased it is wise to take advantage of drop-head models and refuse to accept any other type.

The art of throwing pots

Let us be completely honest right from the beginning of this discussion. You cannot learn to throw a pot by reading about it or looking at diagrams, anymore than you can expect to learn to swim on dry land. However, in both cases, you can quite profitably learn what are the preferred ways to accomplish both these occupations.

If you have a wheel you will be able to both study and practice together and either way you will find the detailed discussion given below, when supported by the sketches, of the greatest value in 'short-cutting' and anticipating many of the difficulties you would otherwise experience.

After some thought as to the best way to assist an understanding of the basic processes in throwing, it appears that the best way is to directly associate the text with a diagram of each step. For this reason the text is to be read with full reference to the appropriate figure for easy understanding.

Preparing the working head: If a drop-head wheel is being used, a plaster bat is a part of the working head. If a flat-topped wheel is used, heavy work can be thrown directly on the head and later cut away with a wire as shown in *Figure 3.3*. Delicate work, liable to easy damage, is better thrown onto a plaster bat which is fixed to the working head with clay pieces – shown diagramatically in *Figure 3.5*. Three clay pellets are disposed more or less equally around the centre of the head. The plaster bat is moistened slightly and worked firmly down on the clay. The head should be spun while this operation is being carried out so that the bat may be centralized and spin true. While there is no real need to have the bat spinning true, the effect of a bat wobbling eccentrically during throwing is most disconcerting.

With the head ready for throwing the real work can begin as follows:

Sketch One: This shows the method of determining the centre of the head prior to the operation of throwing. Rub some really wet clay onto the ball of your thumb. Set the wheel spinning, from right to left (counter-clockwise) is the usual, and press your thumb somewhere in the centre of the head. A well centred print of your thumb will be left.

Sketch Two: Wet your hands from a conveniently situated bowl of water, pick up a sizable ball of clay which has been thoroughly wedged and is in a highly plastic state. Set the wheel in motion. Hold the ball of clay in your two hands, aim at the centre mark on the head and slam the clay hard down as near to the centre mark as possible. If you miss your aiming point by more than a trifle, scrape up the clay, re-wedge and try again. Slamming the clay down hard onto the spinning wheel makes the whole flattened mass adhere firmly to the head and is an essential knack in pot throwing.

Sketch Three: Unless you are exceptionally lucky, you will unfortunately

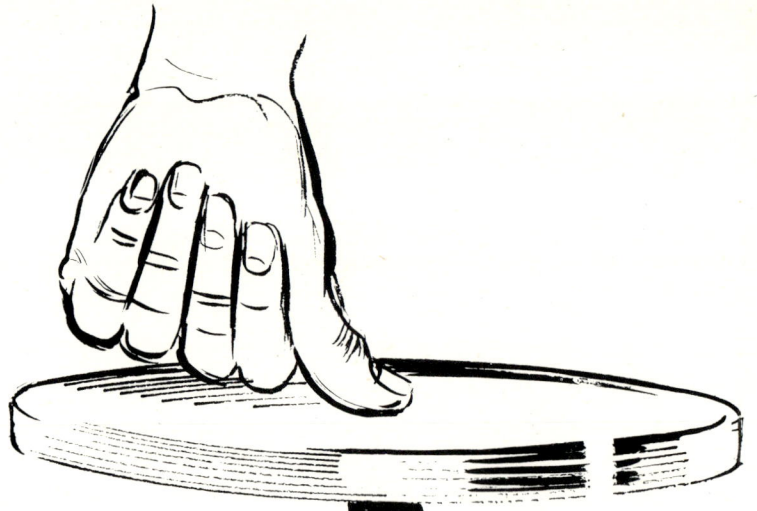

sketch one — finding the centre

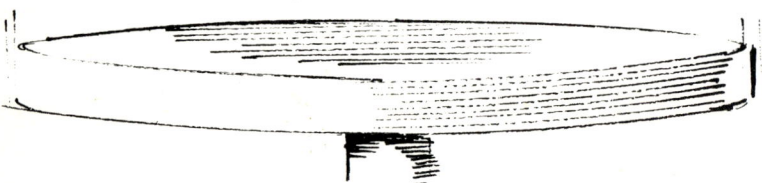

sketch two — throwing on to the wheel

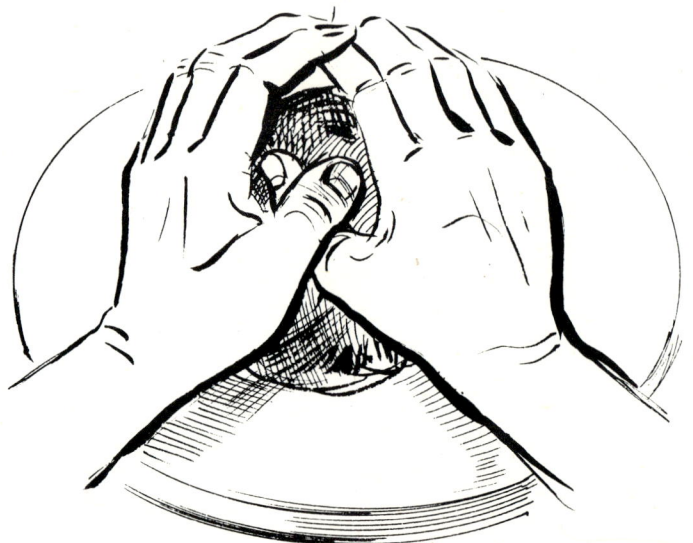

sketch three — centring clay

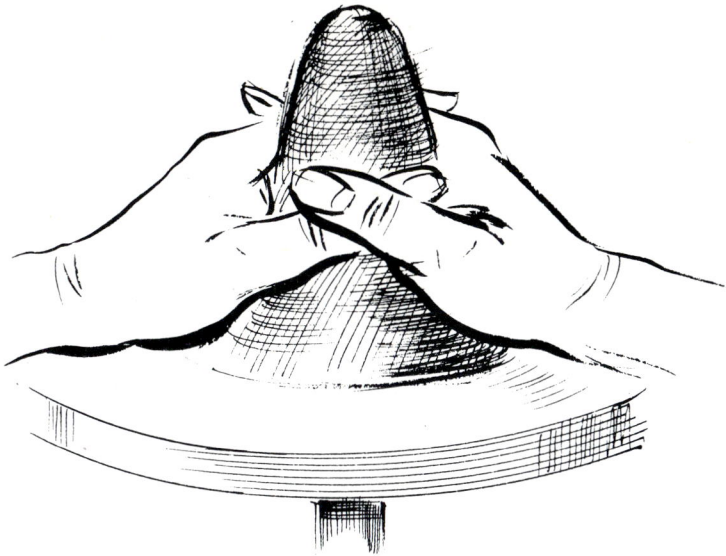

sketch four — working clay up

find that your first few attempts to hit somewhere near the centre of the wheel will be abortive. However, a successful pot cannot be thrown until this process is mastered and it is a case of try, try, try again until for no discernable reason you hit just about right every time. Even though the clay is near centre, the whole mass must be put completely into balance and final centring must be done in this way

(1) Wet your hands well and if necessary squeeze a little water from the sponge over the clay.
(2) Brace your left arm firmly against your body and put the ball of your right hand against the clay. (Some potters prefer to arrange their hands the other way and this is over to the individual.)
(3) Keep the wheel turning rapidly, pull with one hand and push with the opposite hand until the clay is firmly and completely centred on the head.

Note – The description above brings out an absolutely essential point in throwing; one hand must always work against the other. There are no circumstances where pressure, even the slightest pressure, is applied by hand or tool against unsupported clay. Even if only momentary contact is made with the clay with one hand, before the other is offering support, disaster will result.

Sketch Four: To improve the texture of the clay and to ready oneself for the task of creating a shape it is a good idea to work the clay up and down a few times. To raise the clay the hands are locked together around the lump, the heels of the hand exert pressure and it rises between the hands in a tall thin cone.

Sketch Five: To bring the clay back, the heel of the hand is used to press the rotating mass back to its original position. While three sketches have been used to explain the operations of centring, raising, and lowering, these three processes are really all done in the one movement. Beware of overdoing the moving of the clay, as each movement tends to soften the material. Despite this disadvantage of over-softened clay resulting from too much working, a beginner at the art of pot throwing will be wise to practise the above movements in order to perfect the kicking technique with hands, body and feet working together in the rhythm that makes great potters.

sketch five — working clay down

Sketch Six: The next step is to open the centre of the clay in order that the walls can be drawn. The hands must be kept wet in order that the clay be well lubricated. The thumb is used to open the clay as shown in the sketch. The hole is opened until the thumb is inserted to within about ½ an inch of the head.

Note – as the walls rise opposing forces operate:
(a) The pressure of the outside hand tends to push the clay towards the centre and the pressure of the inner hand opposes this force and stops the wall from collapsing inwards
(b) A centrifugal force caused by the rotation of the wheel tends to throw the clay outward. This outward force is a stretching force and if allowed to take control will cause the walls to grow flabby and collapse. The faster the wheel spins, the greater the centrifugal force, and the greater the control needed to be exerted by the outside hand.

Sketch Seven: This sketch shows a further stage in the opening out process. The two hands must really work together from this stage on. The left hand inside the bowl forces the clay outward and upwards. The right hand determines how far the clay moves. The two hands working together determine the thickness of the walls.

Note – It is at this point in raising the walls, that any failure to exactly centre the clay or any inefficiency in preparing the clay with consequent uneven texture, will have resulted in an uneven height to the walls. If this lack of symmetry is serious there is nothing to be done but start from the beginning. If the inbalance is slight it can be corrected by trimming the top using, strangely enough, a stout darning needle, set if you will in a wooden handle. The needle point is made to score the clay all the way through and is much more effective than a knife would be.

Sketch Eight: If the walls of the pot are to be straight the inner hand is kept straight and moves up and down vertically as it follows the fingers of the outside hand as they try to lift a band of clay upwards. Vertical sides are much more difficult to accomplish than sloping sides and much more liable to collapse.

It is at this point that the base must be dealt with. The final thickness of the base must be in proportion to the pot and can only be judged by eye. The thickness of the bottom can be tested by probing through with a needle until the work head is felt. An old spoon, with the lip filed or ground to shape is an excellent implement for cutting away surplus clay from the foot.

sketch six — thumbing centre hole

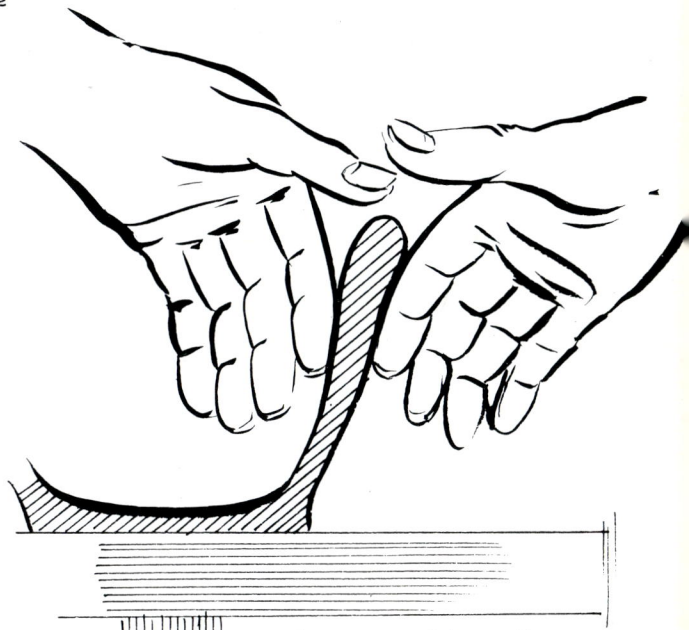

sketch seven — raising walls

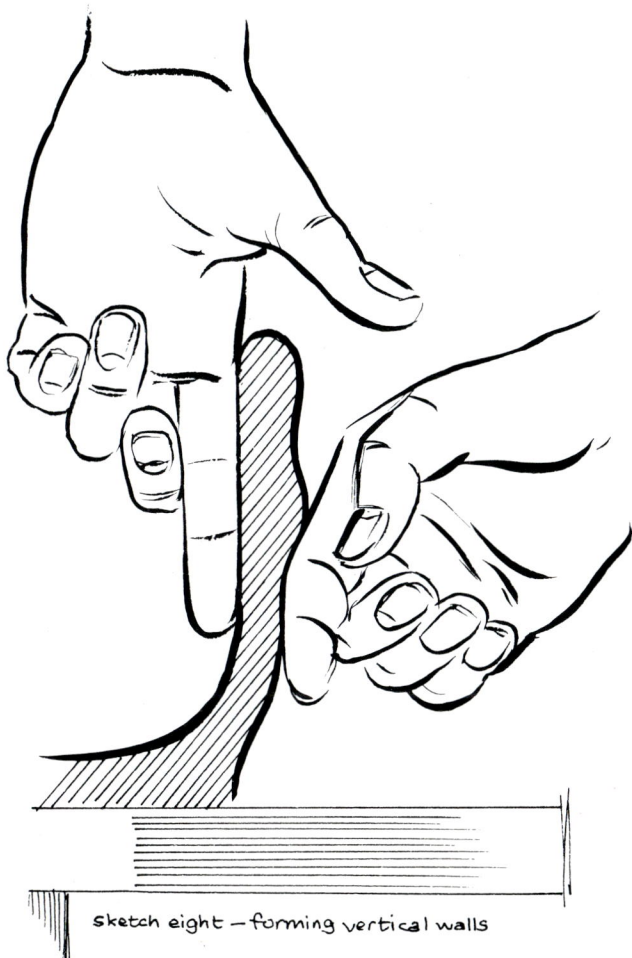

sketch eight — forming vertical walls

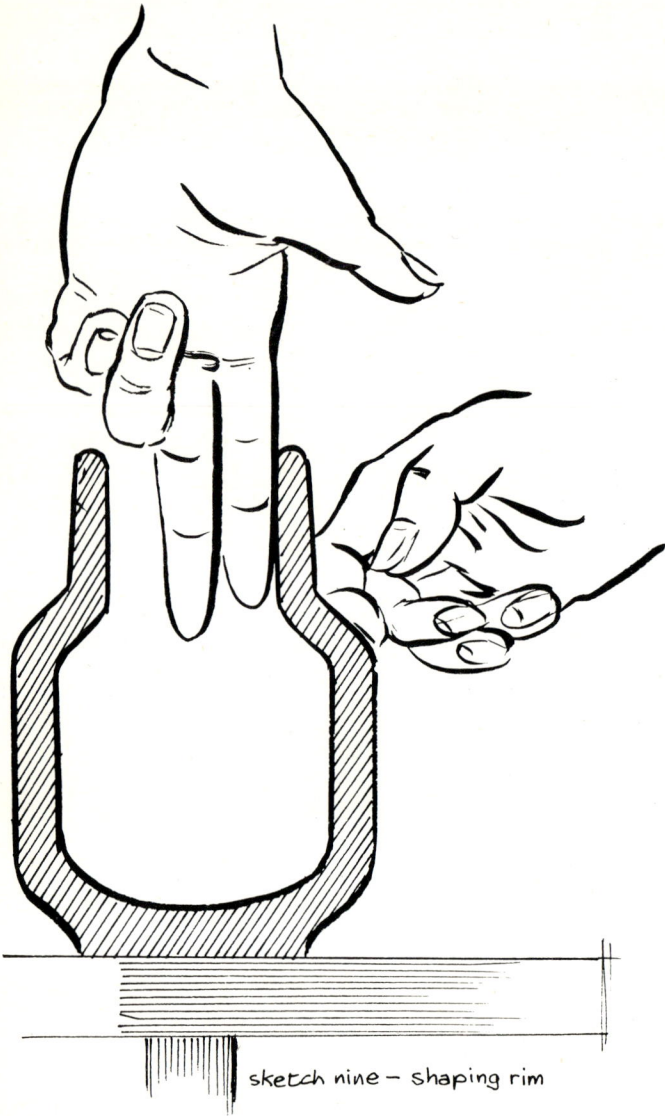

sketch nine — shaping rim

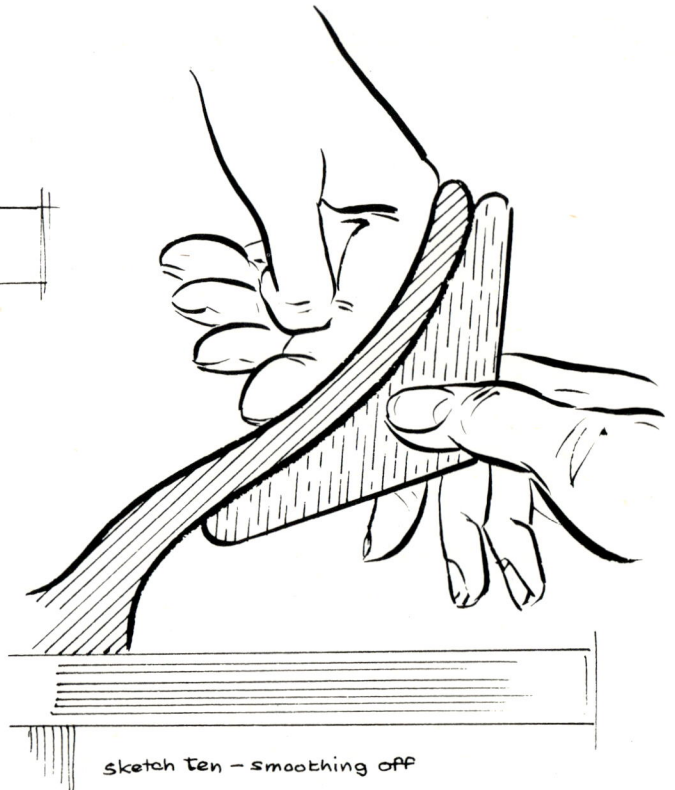

sketch ten — smoothing off

Sketch Nine: The top of the pot must always be finished with care. A distorted rim or uneven height of the walls can be trimmed as suggested above. In most cases the rim should be rather heavier than the walls. A strong rim to a pot will reinforce thin walls most satisfactorily. If the design will stand it a strongly flattened rim is a good insurance against breakage in service and looks well. It is surprising, or perhaps not so after reflection, that those design features which lend natural strength to a structure are aesthetically pleasing. This is the theory of simple design, the primitive growing of a shape in conformity to the natural attributes of the original clay. Bearing this in mind leads always to the clean sweeping lines of a well designed thrown pot.

Sketch Ten: Few are the potters who can bring a bowl or pot to its final finish without the use of a tool. Many potters use a wide variety of scrapers and other tools in an endeavour to obtain the contour they planned. Whether such tools are used or not is an individual preference but it does seem a waste of effort to raise a mass of clay upwards and then be forced to carve it away simply because it is in the wrong place. However, where a number of articles need to conform more or less to a standard size or shape the use of a shaped scraper as in the sketch helps considerably. In other cases a few touches of a wet sponge inside and out should be all that is necessary in order that a pleasantly smooth finish be gained.

And that brings to the end the actual operation of throwing pots on a wheel. To say that a complete description has been given would be to sadly exaggerate. We can only say what we said at the beginning and that is the fact that throwing on a wheel can only be learned by doing it. Practice is essential, many disappointments are inevitable; the above description of processes will have done well if it has reduced the number of failures any potter experiences. We have endeavoured to avoid stating the obvious and this will account for many omissions.

Making spouts

There are a number of processes associated with thrown pottery. One of the most difficult is the making of pouring lips on jugs and pitchers and spouts on teapots and coffee jugs.

A pouring lip is made by supporting the rim with two fingers of one hand while pulling the clay outward with a finger of the other hand. The two fingers squeeze as well as hold while the other hand ends with a downward pinching movement between finger and thumb. The hands must be wet and the rim moistened to prevent cracking. *Figure 3.6* shows diagramatically the preferred shape of an efficient pouring lip.

The downward curve must be sharp and the lower edge needs to be suddenly reduced in thickness if drops of liquid are not to temporarily hang on the lower lip.

The making and setting of spouts is a more complicated procedure. This is demonstrated in *Figure 3.7* and proceeds as follows:

(1) Use normal throwing procedure and raise a tall thin cylinder.
(2) Insert a long round wooden tool into the centre of the cylinder. (A wooden dowel will do.) Stick it well into the clay of the base and allow it to rotate with the work.
(3) Close the top in until a cone is formed and gently work the tool loose from the centre.
(4) Cut the cone with a wet knife on the slant as shown in the diagram.
(5) Open a hole in the appropriate place on the side of the pot. Note the position of the spout as shown in *Figure 3.8.*
(6) Join spout and body together firmly, using the smallest quantity of very wet extra clay. It is perhaps wise to let the spout and pot dry for an hour or so for extra strength and then wet only those parts which will be joined.
(7) Use a round or ball ended tool inside the pot to ensure that a satisfactory join, not blocking the spout is formed on the inside.

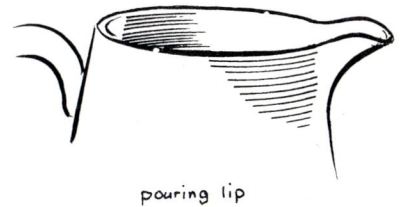

pouring lip

Figure 3.6

Figure 3.7

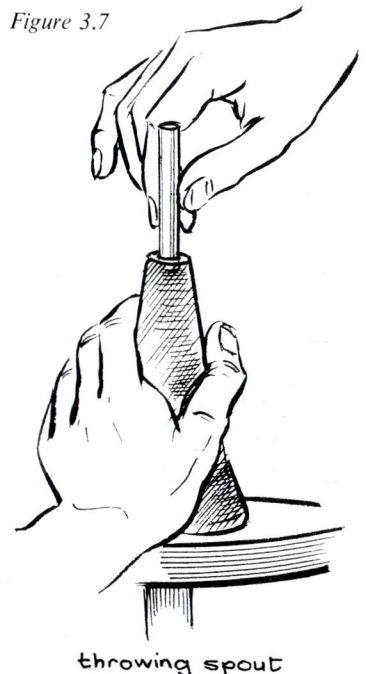

throwing spout

Figure 3.8

fixing spout (inside)

line of spout

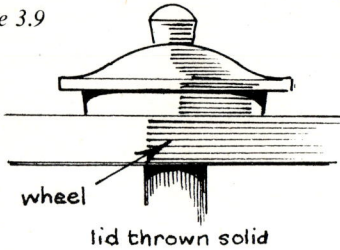

Figure 3.9

wheel

lid thrown solid

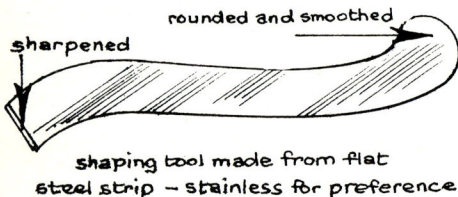

Figure 3.10

rounded and smoothed

sharpened

shaping tool made from flat
steel strip – stainless for preference

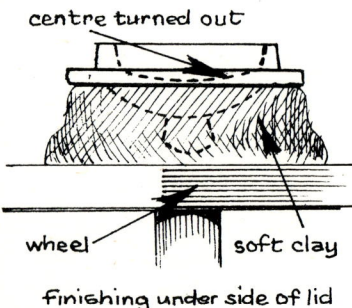

Figure 3.11

centre turned out

wheel   soft clay

finishing under side of lid

(8) Use somewhat the same technique (with a tool instead of a finger) to shape the pouring lip as was described for the jug above.

Teapots have been made in a variety of shapes and spouts to match the shape. It is interesting to experiment with a variety of shapes for the making of teapots but it will be found that the traditional shape as evolved over many years seems to suit itself to the purpose of tea making better than any other. Further proof that functional designs combined with evolution over a period, produce lines which are the most pleasing. And talking about functionalism, do not neglect to make the outlet of the spout higher than any possible level reached within the pot. This is easily overlooked in fixing a spout to a body and results in a pot which may look pleasing but is rather messy to use.

Making lids

One method of making a lid was described in some detail in Chapter 2 but it is possible to produce more pleasing shapes for rounded pots by throwing the lid on the wheel. The complication of throwing a lid comes from both the top and bottom needing to be shaped. *Figure 3.9* shows the first step in the usual way of making such a lid. The lid begins as a solid block of clay and is worked and then cut to shape with a tool such as is shown in *Figure 3.10*. To hold the shape of the horizontal rim on the lid the clay needs to be allowed to stiffen for a time before the sharp edge of the tool is used to cut away the surplus clay.

When the solid lid has dried to the leather stage, it is remounted upside down on the wheel supported by a mound of wet clay and the centre is then turned out as described later in this chapter and shown in *Figure 3.11*. The design of lids must conform to the design of the pot and once again shapes which have evolved over many years of use will be found to be the most acceptable.

Making handles

Refer back to the technique of pulling clay as described in Chapter 2. The thin ropes of clay so made are the starting point for providing any pot with a handle. Little need be said about the very great variation in shape and size which can be incorporated in a handle. The main points to remember in making and attaching handles to pots are four in number and are as follows:

(1) To maintain the balance of a pot the handle must appear as if it had grown out of the pot. Therefore it must be affixed in exactly the right place and there must be harmony between the shape of the pot and the shape of the handle. This harmony includes not only the line of the handle but also the thickness of the handle. Possibly no other operation in pottery making sorts out the true craftsman with an appreciation of balance and form, from the clumsy amateur, as does the fixing of the right handle, in the right place on a pot. Do not misunderstand this last statement. This is not the introduction of an argument of the professional versus the amateur.

Figure 3.12

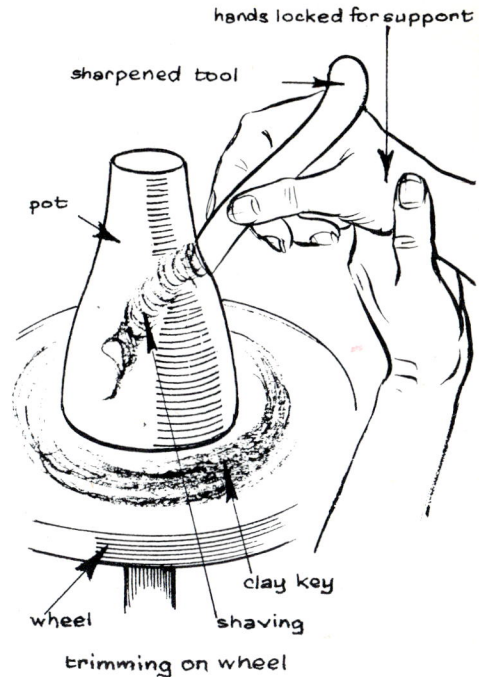

hands locked for support

sharpened tool

pot

wheel

clay key

shaving

trimming on wheel

Quite the contrary. Many of the rankest beginners in the craft of pottery show an innate understanding and appreciation of balance and form which is quite beyond the grasp of some potters with years of experience. This is one of the fascinations of the craft of pottery, this determination and demonstration of abilities one is not conscious of possessing.

(2) As most people know, an awkward overly small handle on a cup, pot or jug is an abomination to the user. Therefore a potter should err on the side of generosity in the size of a handle always within the limits of the design.

(3) A pottery handle in itself is rather stronger than appearances seem to indicate and this is as well for a handle is subject to considerable leverage when lifting a full vessel. However, the stress due to the leverage applies to the joint between the handle and the body to a rather greater extent than to the handle itself. This is fair warning that handles must be fixed with the greatest security possible to the body. Normally this is achieved when the handle flows into the body, rather than nestling coyly on the side. Bear this in mind.

(4) Unless a potter is highly experienced it is wise to allow both the handle and the pot to harden for an hour or so before fixing the handle. Remember that local dampening of the site of the join will bring both handle and pot to a plastic condition again.

Leathering

The term leathering has been used to a considerable extent in previous writing in this book and fairly obviously it is a highly descriptive way of referring to the drying out of the clay after work has been finished. It is now necessary to give a little further thought to this subject. When a pot or other piece is cut loose from the work head of the wheel and placed on a bat to dry, the clay shrinks with the loss of water, turns lighter in colour and becomes surprisingly tough. In this condition the piece can be handled with some confidence.

It is at the leather stage that final trimming to shape, carving and a number of operations are carried out and this will be dealt with now.

Trimming: Trimming on a wheel is a very similar operation to turning wood on a lathe. The piece in its leather stage is centred on the work head and sharp tools of various shapes are used to shave off unwanted parts and to impart incised designs in a similar fashion. The operation is simple to describe but like most other things in the craft of pottery it requires considerable practice to become proficient. The steps are as follows: (*Figure 3.12* shows most of the details.)

(1) The piece is keyed to the work head with plastic clay. Provided the keying clay is not too wet and that the piece is not left in contact for a lengthy period, the clay will not stick to the piece.

(2) The pot may be mounted either the right way up but more usually with the base up, as a good potter strives to finish all but the base during the throwing.

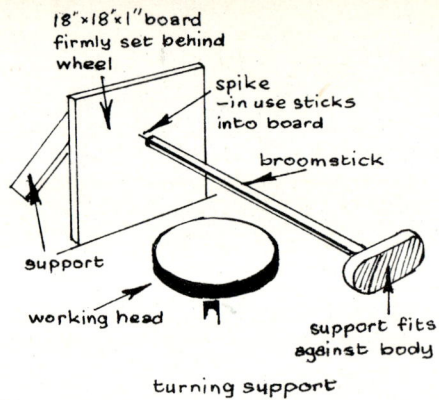

18"×18"×1" board firmly set behind wheel

spike – in use sticks into board

broomstick

Figure 3.13

support

working head

support fits against body

turning support

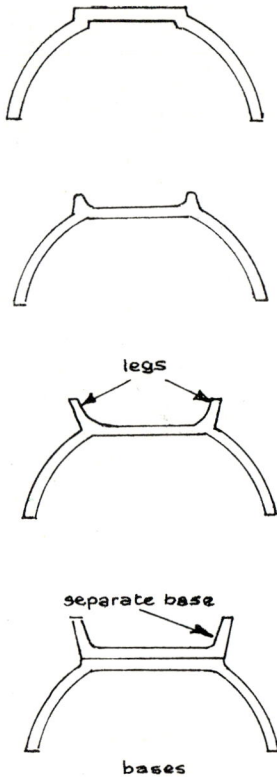

legs

separate base

bases

Figure 3.14

(3) The piece is at the correct leather stage for trimming when the shavings come cleanly away from the tool in long curls; stickiness is proof that the drying time has been too short; a tendency to powder shows that the piece is over-conditioned. Conditioning is carried out in a damp-box described in Appendix B. The use of a damp-box is the most effective way of conditioning, although judicious use of damp cloths inside a large plastic bag holding the piece will do the job if patiently handled.

(4) It is imperative that the trimming tool be correctly shaped for the job in hand. The cutting edge must be sharp and the end slightly inclined in respect to the length of the tool. This bend allows the natural hold on the tool to bring it into contact with the piece at the correct angle to shave away the unwanted portions.

(6) The cutting tool must be held firmly. Experienced potters have learned to lock their hands together as shown in *Figure 3.12* in order to provide a triangular support. It is desirable to adopt this stance if only in the interest of saving time. If this method does not work out or if a particularly delicate operation is to be done, a 'turning support' as shown in *Figure 3.13* can be used.

(7) Merchants offer a very wide selection of tools claimed to be necessary for successful pottery craft. These claims tend to be exaggerated and it is a good general rule to make most tools oneself and then only make them as the demand arises.

(8) Think back to the discussion on the allowable thickness of pottery given in the section on 'grog' in Chapter 2. Applying the principles given there means that in trimming the base of a pot, sufficient must be cut away to reduce all sections of the base within safe limits for firing. The most useful way to do this is to hollow the base. Some suggestions for base shapes are given in *Figure 3.14*.

Note – In all working with clay pieces, either in the making, throwing or trimming, sharp changes of direction must be avoided if possible. If necessary refer back to the section in Chapter 2 where the stresses set up in the clay body during firing were discussed. An appreciation of that discussion is important for there is a great temptation to produce sharp corners, both internal and external when trimming. Particularly, sharp internal corners (as can happen where base meets body) are liable to lead to fracture during firing.

Two piece pots

It is not the intention of this book to lead on to complicated techniques in the craft of pottery. Certainly there are plenty of advanced methods of handling clay, ways of the potter that are fascinatingly creative, but such techniques will be the subject of a further volume in this series, so reserving this book for the basic procedures. Despite this resolution, there is one way of producing highly complicated looking ware, with a technique that is simple and employs no great advance on anything that has been discussed so far. The reference is to the two piece pot.

With small necked pots, of which wine jugs or bottles, depicted in *Figure 3.15* are typical examples, it is not easy to fully control the throwing of

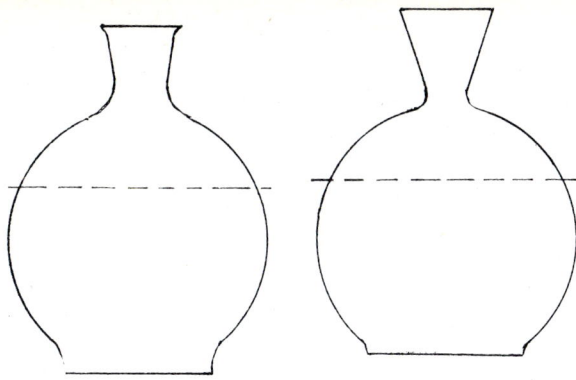

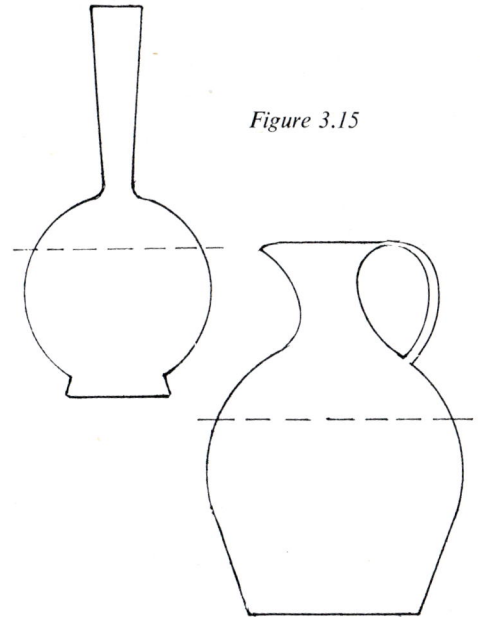

Figure 3.15

the walls without extensive experience.

The means of overcoming such difficulties have been used at least since the time of the Etruscans for pots from this period are known to be made from the joining of two separately thrown parts.

No new techniques are introduced in throwing each half separately. There are a few points that need to be watched and these are as follows:

(1) This is a case where it is desirable to have a full size sketch of the final design. With this to hand the point of juncture between the two parts can be determined and the walls of each part raised to the desired height and direction of sweep of the form at that point.

(2) The trimming of the base will be more difficult owing to greater height and complexity of the finished form and a solid base, cut during the throwing stages, should be used.

(3) The rim of one part must exactly match the rim of the other part and to ensure this callipers of some sort are needed. Such callipers can be two thin shaped strips of wood fastened together as shown in *Figure 3.16*, and used as depicted thereon. A rim can be expanded to size by ordinary methods of drawing out as used in throwing. To contract the diameter of the rim it is advisable to cut some of the rim back to a smaller diameter.

(4) To ensure a joint that will not open either during drying or firing, it is vital to have both parts in exactly the same stage of drying. For this reason the one processed piece of clay should be done in the one work period and the pieces should be placed side by side for partial drying.

(5) The rims should be made to partly interlock as shown in *Figure 3.17* and the channel piece flooded with a liquid mixture of clay in water (slip). The two parts may be carefully seated and the wheel spun gently while the top part is tapped gently into place while the extra clay on the overhang of the lower rim is worked gently into place. It is obvious that the parts must be in a suitable condition of firmness or the pot will collapse at this stage.

(6) The base of the top part should have been kept slightly moist while the rest of the piece partially dries. This can be done by wrapping with a piece of plastic film to prevent evaporation of the water. If moist enough, what was previously the base can now be drawn to the shape of the neck making an interior opening into the lower part with a suitable tool.

(7) With a small piece of wet sponge tied to a long wire, the inside of the joint can be smoothed off by inserting through the neck. The jug can now be finished as if it had been thrown in one piece.

Making two piece pots requires a measure of control and accuracy which can only come from practice with lesser pieces. It is surprising though just how soon a tyro-potter can reach the desired standard to carry out this method of pot making with every expectation of success.

That just about covers the essentials of the fascinating art of 'throwing'. Perhaps it would be kind to warn busy people to give consideration to the time they can afford to expend on a craft. For fascinating is the correct word and once some proficiency has been gained in the art of throwing it is difficult not to neglect other occupations in favour of throwing more and more and more pots.

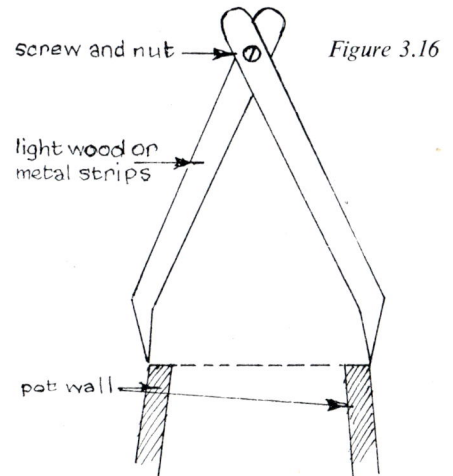

screw and nut

Figure 3.16

light wood or metal strips

pot wall

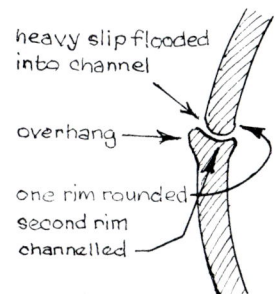

Figure 3.17

heavy slip flooded into channel

overhang

one rim rounded

second rim channelled

CHAPTER FOUR

Moulding clay

Moulding is standard practice in the mass production of pottery ware. A modern ceramics factory will have hundreds of moulds each capable of turning out thousands of identical pieces of pottery ware each week. The creativity in such ware is restricted to the original master from which the mould is cut or cast and such techniques, while of the utmost economic importance, do not come within the scope of this book.

There is, however, a place for the moulding of clay in creating individual pottery pieces and this aspect will be examined in this chapter.

Decorative Panels

An art form of really exciting possibilities and one which fits so well into contemporary architecture is the production of panels in fired clay. Panels are really an arrangement of individual tiles discussed in Chapter 2 but discussion has been left to this chapter because of the repetitive nature of forming the basic form.

In most cases a decorative panel must be of large size; that is, large in length and breadth. The limitations on practical thickness of a clay slab as considered in Chapter 2 still apply and it may be as well to add to what was said there.

When clay is heated to a high temperature the physical components of the clay undergo a chemical change. Pure clay is composed of alumina (Al_2O_3), silica (S_1O_2) and chemically combined water (H_2O) making up a substance called hydrous aluminium silicate with the chemical formula ($Al_2O_3 — 2SiO_2 — 2H_2O$). This formula is the chemists' way of saying that one part of alumina is combined with two parts of silica and two parts of water. The two parts of water are the 'stumbling block' in firing thick clay slabs. The water in this case is not water which has been added to make clay plastic. On the contrary, it is water which is so intimately combined with the other two constituents in clay that a piece of clay heated to any temperature below the firing point, and hence by all tests perfectly dry, still retains two parts water. This is common to many substances which contain chemically combined water (water which is not detectable by ordinary tests).

On heating strongly, clay releases this chemically combined water and becomes pottery. This loss of the water constituent of hydrous aluminium silicate is one of the most significant changes which takes place during firing. As we are all aware, if water is heated strongly in an enclosed space, tremendous steam pressures build up and can eventuate in an explosion. Precisely this state of affairs will exist within a pottery piece during firing. Unless the water has an escape route, pressure will build up and the pottery will shatter under the internal pressure of trapped water. Not only will that piece be ruined but adjacent pieces in the kiln may also be damaged.

The obvious way to avoid an explosion within the kiln is to allow escape routes for the release of the chemically combined water as firing proceeds.

(1) This can be done through keeping pottery walls, bases and bodies sufficiently thin to allow easy egress of moisture through the natural pores

Figure 4.1

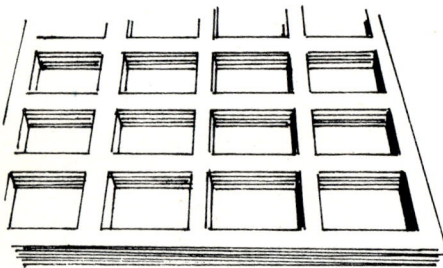

open honeycomb structure giving strength to large flat panel of the material. For this reason it is normal practice to hollow out bases of pots and other articles and to build any but the smallest sculptures with hollow centres.

(2) Another way is to introduce extra porous material into the body of the clay to make artificial escape paths for the water. Such material is most conveniently 'grog' or clay that has been fired to a high enough temperature to allow its chemically combined water to escape but to an insufficiently high temperature to cause the other materials in the clay to fuse together and make the clay waterproof. Flower pots for instance are fired to the point where they are porous, whereas earthenware is fired well into the temperature where the other constituents flow together and make the pot wholly watertight. From this it follows that broken up flower pots, or any other clay fired into that condition, make usable grog but ground up earthenware is liable to be completely useless for this purpose.

We can now return to the consideration of how the above facts will affect the design of large clay panels. Actually the difficulty in design resolves itself into two opposing characteristics of clay and pottery.

(1) A solid clay panel is liable to break or at the least distort in firing if it is too thick. The maximum thickness will depend on the characteristics of the clay used. A highly plastic, easily worked clay may distort or break if thicker than about $\frac{1}{2}$ an inch while a more sandy clay, stiff to work and difficult to handle may possibly fire out well in thicknesses up to $1\frac{1}{2}$ inches. A little reflection in consideration of the facts discussed above will show why sandy clay is more able to fire out well than purer clay.

(2) While the needs of firing require comparative thin panels, such panels will lack mechanical strength, for pottery is inherently unable to withstand bending or shock of any kind.

These two opposing requirements can be resolved by any of the following three major techniques:

(1) Make a thick panel and heavily grog the clay body. The amount of grog required can only be judged by actual trial and error and with large pieces this is a little clumsy through having to make up test pieces to actual size. Large quantities of grog tend to defeat the reason for grogging to some extent for an 'over-grogged' panel will be mechanically weak.

(2) To mould panels with the rear of the panel in the shape of an open honey comb. (*Figure 4.1*.) Such a structural shape will add great strength to the panel and still allow all sections to be comparatively thin. This unquestionably is the most elegant way of making a panel and in some cases the structural shapes can be incorporated into the design on the face of the panel. However, another practical consideration comes into effect at this point, the question of whether the kiln is large enough to accommodate a large piece. If the potter has a large kiln then this type of reinforcement, the making of which is described below, should be given every consideration.

(3) Probably the most practical solution and one which most potters will be forced to adopt is to cut the large panel into smaller, tile size pieces and after firing, reassemble them onto a concrete slab backing. This method does introduce some complications, and the design used will have to conform to some extent to the need to break the panel into smaller elements.

Whatever method of handling the completed panel is adopted, there are certain preliminaries which must be undertaken in common and these are as follows:

(1) A flat surface, at least as large as the size of the complete panel must be available and free to allow the panel to be undisturbed for at least 48 hours after moulding.

(2) The panel design may be of any shape; square, rectangular, round, oval, or free form. Free form panels of a shape determined by the imagination (some of which are shown in *Figure 4.2*) conform particularly well to the innate quality of plasticity in clay.

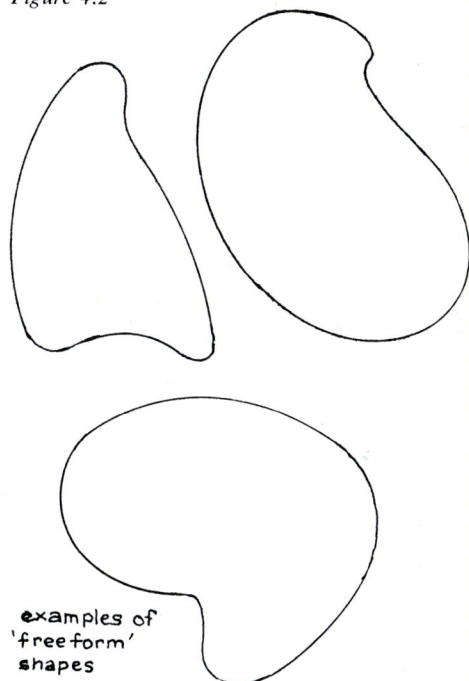

Figure 4.2

examples of 'free form' shapes

Figure 4.3

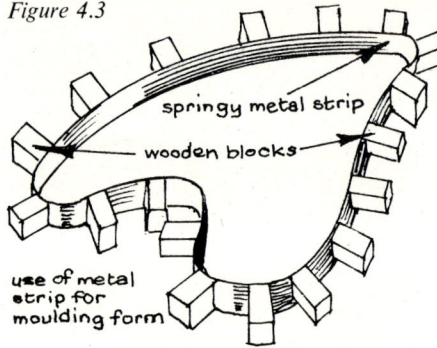

use of metal strip for moulding form

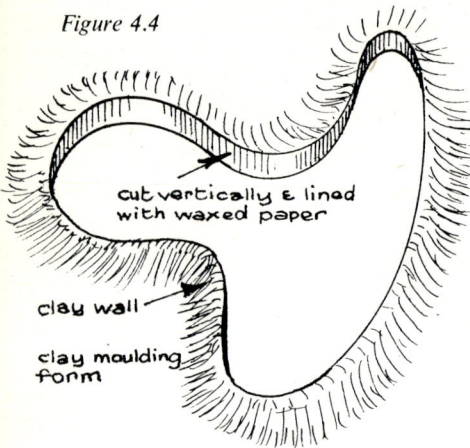

Figure 4.4

cut vertically & lined with waxed paper

clay wall

clay moulding form

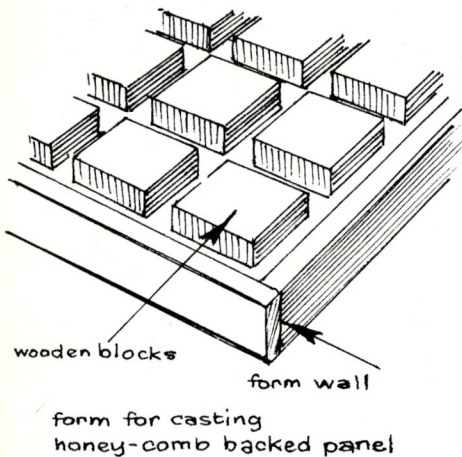

Figure 4.5

wooden blocks

form wall

form for casting honey-comb backed panel

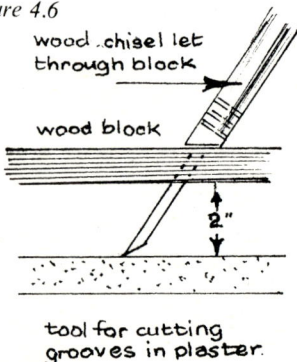

Figure 4.6

wood chisel let through block

wood block

2"

tool for cutting grooves in plaster.

(3) A form-work or frame must be made to follow the outline of the proposed panel. For square or oblong shapes the form can be made of 1 inch by 1 inch dressed timber, tacked in place by lightly nailing to the working surface. For curved and irregular shapes a length of metal strip, at least 2 inches in width can be flexed around a series of wooden blocks tacked to the working surface. (*Figure 4.3*). Alternately, a wall of clay can be formed to follow the shape, the vertical inside surface of the wall being lined with wax paper or other impervious flexible material during the operation of moulding the panel. (*Figure 4.4*). With the more complicated shapes, a length of stiff rope can be dropped into the approximate position of the form walls where it will drop into natural curves and these curves can be followed in making the form walls.

From this point on the technique has to vary in accordance with the treatment of the panel.

(4) For a flat back panel, either thick or thin, the interior of the form should be covered with powdered grog or similar fine powder. This is to prevent the clay from sticking to the working surface and cracking as it shrinks through drying.

(5) To form a honeycomb base two alternative methods of forming the honeycombs can be used:

(i) A series of wooden blocks can be tacked to the working surface as shown in *Figure 4.5*. These blocks can be say 2 inches by 2 inches by 2 inches and should be spaced $\frac{3}{4}$ inch apart.

(ii) Three inches in thickness of plaster of Paris can be cast into the form and then cut carefully with $\frac{3}{8}$ inch or $\frac{3}{4}$ inch grooves at $2\frac{1}{4}$ inch centres to form a honeycomb section. A tool can be made as in *Figure 4.6* from a suitable wood chisel to expedite this cutting. Good quality plaster should be used and finally when all plaster dust has been completely brushed away the whole of the interior should be brushed over with a light coating of grease. Clear lubricating grease or petroleum jelly dissolved in gasoline will make a liquid which can then be brushed on. The form walls must in both cases be high enough to allow of $\frac{1}{2}$ inch of solid panel above the honeycomb.

Well wedged heavily grogged clay in a highly plastic state is now used to form the panel whether flat or honeycombed backed. The procedure is as follows:

(1) With wet hands work clay into lumps and press a series of these lumps into the form, carefully overlapping and working each successive lump into the main mass and filling well into all cavities. This is particularly important with a honeycomb panel.

(2) The hands must be kept wet, the clay very plastic, rather wetter than is used for other clay forming techniques and great importance is attached to excluding all air bubbles.

(3) As each section, starting from one end, is filled, a solid and heavy block of flat wood is used to pound and beat the clay slab to ensure complete consolidation of the clay in the slab.

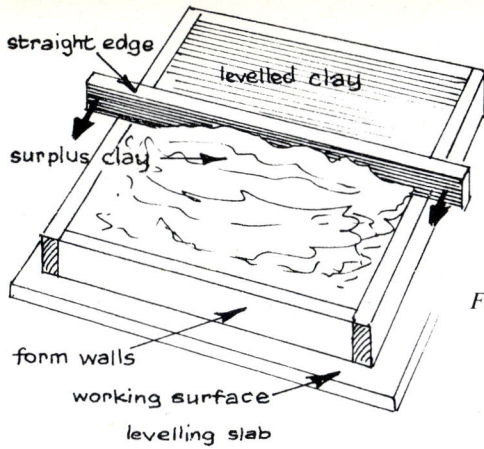

Figure 4.7

Figure 4.8

wood strip

height of clay
form walls

wooden blocks
screwed or
nailed to straight
edge

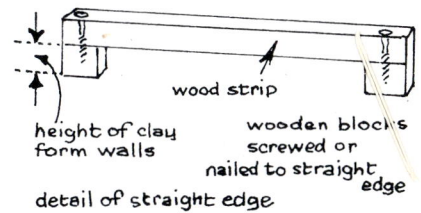

detail of straight edge

levelling slab where clay form
walls are used

(4) Where strips of wood of even thickness have been used for the form walls, a straight edge riding on the form walls (*Figure 4.7*) is used to make sure the slab surface is level. If clay or other irregular height walls are used, a tool as shown in *Figure 4.8* will do the job.

The slab can be left to dry without further disturbance until the leather stage is reached and then decorated in any of the variety of ways discussed in Chapter 5.

An interesting possibility to produce both a reinforced slab and a deeply incised decorative panel is to reverse the technique described above in making a honeycomb panel. The design for the front of the panel is incised deeply into the plaster or blocked out with wooden blocks tacked to the working surface. The panel is then moulded upside down. The fact that the design is now to act also as a structural reinforcement must not be lost sight of, neither should the need to ensure no section be greater than ¾ of inch through. With these requirements in mind there still remain some fascinating possibilities in moulding really striking panels.

Where a large thin panel is to be cut into smaller pieces for later re-assembly, a potter will find that in most cases irregular cuts will be more appropriate to the design than cutting into regular squares. (*Figure 4.9*). Not only will non-straight cuts fit better into the design but each tile will be keyed to its neighbour, rather like a jig-saw puzzle, for easy re-assembly. The cutting of the slab should be delayed until the decoration is applied or at least until the design is laid out on the surface. Then the cutting can be done with a sharp firm bladed knife held vertically.

The making of pottery panels is a highly rewarding pursuit, both in results achieved and in the demand apparent for panels. A potter considering using his craft for semi-commercial ends, thus obtaining some financial return for his skill and artistic ability, is well advised to explore the demand for pottery panels. There are at present few panel makers offering their wares and there are signs of an increasing demand on a worldwide scale for panels made from fired clay.

While decorative floor or wall panels offer the greatest scope for individual non-repetitive artistry in moulding techniques, this is not to say that other moulded objects are not aesthetic in value. A few other moulding techniques are therefore discussed below.

Press-in moulds
Normally used as an aid to the duplication of one design, the method of using press-in moulds for the initial shaping of clay pieces has some merit. The production of the press-in mould itself is not difficult and proceeds thus:

(1) The starting point of the mould is a solid clay master form. This is simply a lump of clay brought to the correct shape by pressing, throwing, incising or sculpturing. It produces in solid form an exact duplicate of the lines and form of the article to be made.
(2) In considering the design of the master form it is well to bear in mind

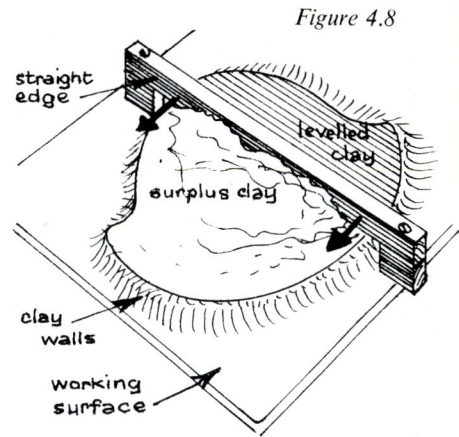

Figure 4.9

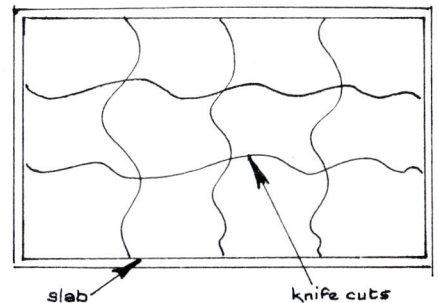

cutting slab into irregular
shaped tiles

Figure 4.10

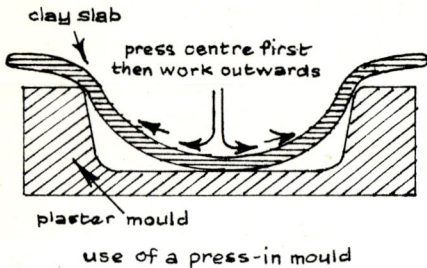

clay slab

press centre first
then work outwards

plaster mould

use of a press-in mould

that it is not a pattern for a mass-produced article that is being built but a form, simple in shape, clean of line, with no acute angles and of no great symmetry from which will be made an individual piece of pottery.

(3) On a flat smooth, non-porous surface (a sheet of glass or plastic or a piece of well varnished board) build up the clay master form, using fairly stiff clay in the centre and plastic clay on the outside. The inclusion of air bubbles is of no importance but a good profile shape is.

(4) Allow the clay to dry to firmness and complete the outer surface by scraping. See that there is no overhang in the design that could prevent the master form from coming free from the mould.

(5) Build a wall around the master form as suggested in the section on panels. Keep the walls an inch or so clear of the master form.

(6) Mix up a batch of plaster of Paris as described in Appendix A, and pour over the master form and then fill the rest of the space with plaster. Allow the plaster to harden fully.

(7) Remove the master form from the mould; discard the clay. Note – any clay contaminated with plaster of Paris is of no use for pottery. Wash the plaster mould well with cold water.

(8) Take a slab of rolled clay which has been prepared in the same way as for slab pots in Chapter 2. Lay across the mouth of the mould and working from the centre outwards, press the clay firmly into the mould. (*Figure 4.10*. Cut surplus clay around the top of the mould with a wire or knife.

(9) With wet fingers and sponge, round off the edges of the dish and smooth off the bottom and sides.

(10) While the dish is still supported by the mould, carry out any decorative work on the inside of the dish. This support is one of the major reasons for using a mould and allows of quite elaborate incised or sprig moulded (see next section which deals with sprig moulding) decorations of the surface.

(11) The dish is left within the mould until by natural shrinkage it pulls away from the plaster. In this state it can be handled without damage.

The finished cast dish can either be laid aside for decorating or it can be placed in the damp box until sufficiently plastic for further shaping. If the latter procedure is adopted a great variety of individual pieces can be made from the same basic form, each in the same mould.

Sprig moulding

Wedgwood China is world renowned and much of the Wedgwood Company's reputation came from the raised figures and ornaments applied to the outside of Wedgwood pottery pieces. The system devised by Josiah Wedgwood, the founder of the firm, which bears his name, is a simple way whereby a potter can apply decorations of a type not otherwise obtainable. These delicate little clay ornaments are made in a small adaptation of a press mould in which clay is pressed between two half moulds. These tiny moulds are known as 'sprig moulds' and are made as follows:

Figure 4.11

master form

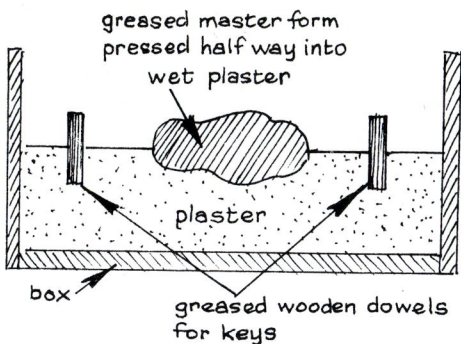

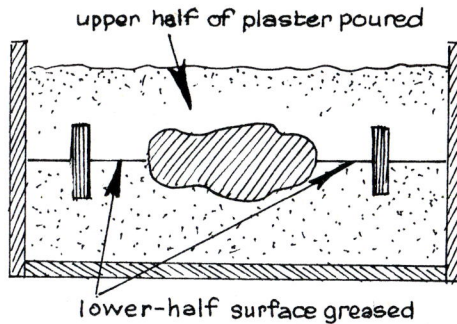

greased master form pressed half way into wet plaster

plaster

box

greased wooden dowels for keys

upper half of plaster poured

lower-half surface greased

Figure 4.11

(1) Before a sprig mould can be made some knowledge of press moulding is advisable. In simple terms a press mould is a two-piece mould in which small clay figures are moulded. The figures must be small, for the essence of press moulding is the production of solid clay pieces. The complete operation is shown in *Figure 4.11* and step by step the procedure is as follows:

(i) Model in clay the required figure to use as a master form.
(ii) Let the master form become dry, touch up and grease well.
(iii) Half fill a box with plaster and before it sets, place the master form to half its depth into the soft plaster.
(iv) Put two well greased lengths of dowel half-way into plaster to act as keys to position the upper section of mould on lower section.
(v) Grease the surface of the solid plaster.
(vi) Pour the upper half of the mould and allow to harden.
(vii) Remove the upper mould and master form.
(viii) Cut a groove or trough around outline on top mould. Tools as used for linoleum cutting will handle this job well. The edge between the mould and the groove is left sharp.
(ix) Put a lump of highly plastic clay in lower mould. Position the upper mould by means of the dowel keys and press firmly down onto bottom mould. The plastic clay will flow to fill both upper and lower mould sections and the excess flow over into the groove.
(x) Leave the mould to dry for a few minutes and then the top mould can be lifted clear and the figure left to dry until it has shrunk clear of the plaster in the lower section.

A sprig mould is made exactly as the above except on a much smaller scale. The use of a sprig mould allows of a motif to be repeated endlessly.

It is quite usual not to use a master form in press and sprig moulding but to incise a design by hand into the surface of the mould halves. This is particularly effective for making abstract decorations and stylised plant forms.

Pressure moulds are commonly used in producing repetitive articles on a small scale. They have a legitimate place in the repertoire of the most individualistic potter for the production of small articles where it is essential to the design to have a motif exactly duplicated. It is also an effective way to make such items as buttons. The holes in the button for threading can be made when the clay is in the half-hard condition by using a coarse needle or similar implement.

Mushroom moulds
Out of the great variety of moulding techniques still left to be discussed, the only one to be further considered in this book is the mushroom mould, virtually the opposite of the press-in mould.

A mushroom mould is cast in a clay master mould which is very similar to an actual press-in mould except instead of a clay slab being pressed

completed lower half of mould

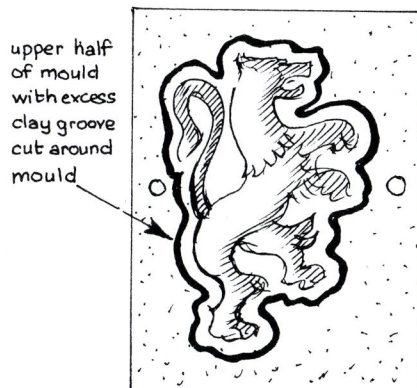

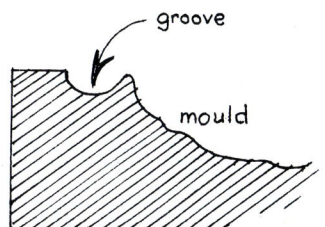

upper half of mould with excess clay groove cut around mould

groove

mould

cross section detail of excess clay groove

Figure 4.12

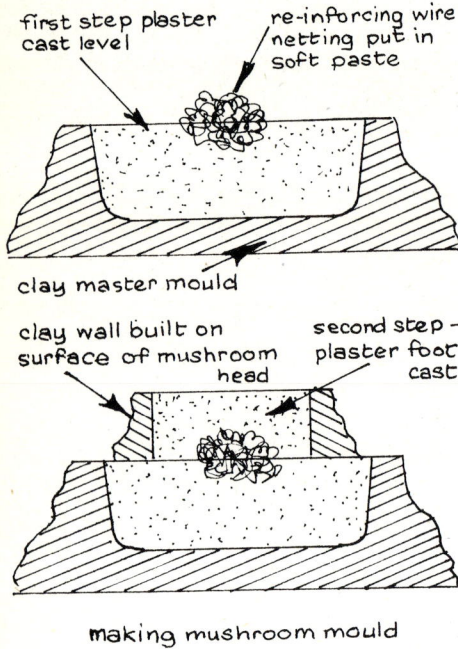

first step plaster
cast level

re-inforcing wire
netting put in
soft paste

clay master mould

clay wall built on
surface of mushroom
head

second step –
plaster foot
cast

making mushroom mould

Figure 4.13

mushroom mould
clay slab moulded over mushroom

surplus clay cut away here

using mushroom mould

Figure 4.14

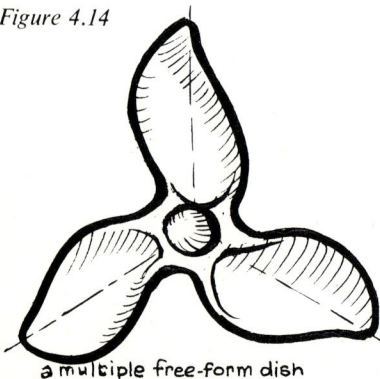

a multiple free-form dish

into a plaster mould, plaster is cast into a clay mould. Incised decorations can be made in the surface of the master mould and will be faithfully transferred in reverse onto the surface of the plaster. *Figure 4.12* shows the casting of the mushroom mould. The details of the operation are as follows:

(i) A lump of clay is hollowed out on a level surface to the desired shape of a dish or other object. The walls of what is now a clay mould are brought level, using a straight edge as depicted in *Figure 4.8*.

(ii) Plaster is cast into the mould and levelled off with the straight edge.

(iii) A crumpled piece of wire-netting or other metal mesh is pushed half-way into the plaster before the plaster hardens.

(iv) The area around the netting is roughened by deeply scratching with a steel tool and a clay fence to contain the foot is raised on the hardened plaster surface. This wall is levelled by extending the blocks on the straight edge.

(v) Plaster is poured for the foot and levelled with the straight edge. The whole mould is left to harden.

To use the mushroom mould, a slab of plastic clay is moulded around the head as shown in *Figure 4.13*. The excess clay can be cut away using a needle rather than a knife.

The mushroom mould lends itself to quickly making nearly identical dishes in a wide variety of shapes. In particular it enables multiple free form dishes to be made where it would be difficult to obtain sufficient likeness between the elements in any other way. An example of this type of dish is illustrated in *Figure 4.14*.

Hollow Sculpture

Small sculptured pieces can be made solid, but larger pieces must be hollow, to prevent breaking during firing. Both press-in moulds and mushroom moulds lend themselves admirably to making the basic body shapes as the starting point for hollow sculptures. For simple sculptures, one mould can make the right and left hand section of say an animal's body. For some complicated sculptures, a right and a left hand mould will need to be used. When two halves of a hollow sculpture have been moulded and allowed to become dry enough to handle with ease, the halves are joined as described for two piece pottery in Chapter 3. In this way a hollow body is made and legs, head, tail and other appendages can be added using a similar technique.

Very large sculptures can be made in this way, the head, legs and tail as well as the body can be made hollow and thus leave no portion of the piece sufficiently thick to be liable to explode in the firing.

As was said earlier in this chapter, most of the moulding techniques are used for repetitive work. However, moulding clay does allow of the convenient creation of non-repetitive articles which might otherwise not be possible. Moulded pottery is different from that made by the other methods described in this book and it can have its own particular appeal. Moulded pottery can be made smoother and lighter in weight with thinner walls than slab or coiled pottery. To try to make a piece of moulded pottery look other than what it is, is very difficult and not worth the trouble. The temptation with moulds is to make the articles over-elaborate and this is self defeating. Remember that simplicity carries with it its own appeal; an aesthetic satisfaction that cannot be achieved with fussiness.

If you have read with understanding as far as this, the time has come to say:

"Welcome to the family of potters, that fraternity of humans who from the most earthy of all substances can extract a little of what is closer to the divine than of the earth, earthy."

Clay, which you have taken as your substance resulted from countless centuries of wind and rain, of frost and sun, to be laid ready to your hand, your skill, your inspiration. Be prepared to spend a few hours of your time, to learn to create objects worthy of that inspiration that rises from within you.

CHAPTER FIVE

Practical pottery decoration

Surface enrichment is an apt technical way to describe carving, incising, scratching, pressing, modelling, painting, dipping, overlaying and many more operations that add character, decorative value and aesthetic appeal to the products of a potter's skill.

To cover the whole field of pottery decoration would be a near impossible task. From the dry-looking unglazed earthen pots of the true primitive, to the fatty glazed colours of Persian style pottery, from the elaborate design of Majolica ware to the abstract art of the contemporary potter, there is a near infinity of possible combinations of colour, texture, design and balance available to the serious potter. Many books on pottery recommend visits to Museums, Art Galleries and pottery exhibitions in order that a potter may steep himself in tradition and gain inspiration from the work of others. Admirable as this advice may be it is certainly not essential; it may even be inhibiting in preventing a potter finding what is truly himself. Certainly when the inner creativity of a potter has been extracted and so as to speak crystalized, is time enough to study, compare and arrange in the light of his own achievements, the products of others.

Principles in decoration

An artist is a fortunate creature. He has achieved a way of expressing inner convictions to an external world, a way of communicating aspirations, meaning and feeling to others outside himself. His duty is the exposure of himself. Personal prejudices and egotistical leanings should not be allowed to envelop a writer but are very difficult to suppress. It seems apposite to mention this matter of prejudice here and now to explain an abborance for the over-elaborate which has been displayed before in this book and comes to a climax in this discussion.

Unquestionably tastes vary; some folk enjoy the gayness of decoration which gives a gypsy-like quality to some pottery. Others prefer plainer ware. Who is to say is right and who is wrong. However, far too often a really beautiful piece of pottery is ruined by over-elaborate ornamentation. The classical lines of a pot which has beneath the hands of a potter grown naturally from the material from which it is made, cannot be improved by elaborate embellishment. When a doubt arises as to whether a certain type of decoration should be applied to a particular piece – the answer is an unequivocally given 'don't'.

A piece of pottery should never serve as a background for decoration. If it is not beautiful in itself, it will at least make grog for a piece that may stand alone on its own merits. Certainly many an excellent piece is given more character, more style, and will become more enchanting by the restrained use of decoration, but until one has gained the experiences to denote one's own individual taste, decoration should be modest indeed. Nevertheless tastes differ and there are even people who will accept factory produced plates and other crockery and, with considerable personal satisfaction, paint their own designs upon them.

Because a choice has to be made among the very numerous classes of

Figure 5.1

scratched designs

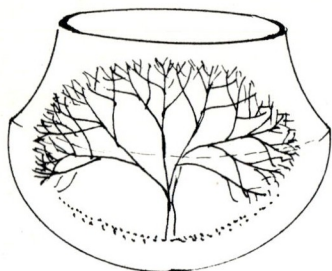

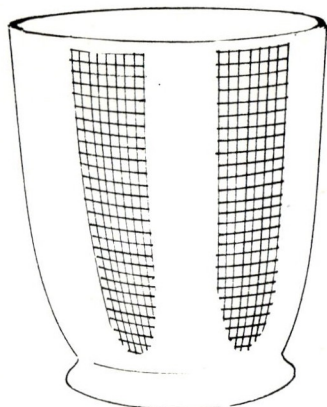

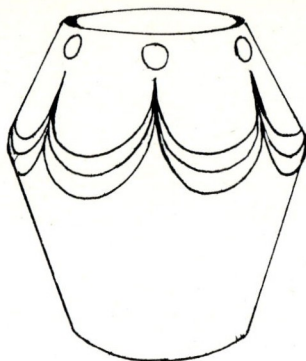

decoration which might be discussed here, and because of the above conviction that simplicity in decoration should be the keynote, only a selection of the plainer types of decorative techniques will be considered.

Decorating plastic clay
The impressions of fingers and thumb marks left from handling and working clay can in some cases be accentuated and incorporated as part of the final finish. While in the plastic state the clay will take impressions readily and the surface can be impressed with stamps of various patterns, scratching, incising, and other surface markings. Because the clay is so plastic any markings made in the surface at this stage will tend to have fluid, liquid-like qualities which can be most attractive. Possibly one of the greatest attractions of applying decoration in the plastic stage is the ease with which mistakes can be modelled out either with fingers or with a flat tool.

Decorating leather hard clay
The usual stage for working the surface of a pot is in the leather state. The pot can be handled with confidence, being strong enough not to distort, the surface will not take finger marks, but is soft enough to work with tools. Scratched designs are about as simple a way of decorating pottery as is possible and perhaps for this reason complement the balance and simplicity of natural forms. Some possibilities are suggested in *Figure 5.1*.

Applied decoration
At the leather stage applied decoration can be added. Sprigs, the small moulded pieces made in the sprig moulds in Chapter 4, are moulded to the surface by using a thick slip as an adhesive and dampening the surface of both the body and the sprig and liberally applying slip between the two; precautions as discussed previously over joining clay apply to fixing of applied decorations.

Sprigs are only one of a number of ways of making the small pieces for applied decoration. Simple shapes can be cut directly from a thin plastic slab made as in Chapter 2 while sprig moulding is reserved for more complicated shapes which might be more difficult to mould by hand. *Figure 5.2* indicates a few possibilities in applied decoration. Looking at these four examples, it would seem that the fish shown at 'C' could be sprig moulded, and possibly the round shapes in 'A', while the embellishment in 'D', where only one is required, would be separately carved.

Carved decoration
Whereas applied decoration is a method of building up the surface, carving involves cutting it away. Carving is particularly satisfactory for lightening the appearance of an over-heavy pot. Pottery lamp bases are effective vehicles for the use of carved decoration as the shaded light from above will throw into relief carved features and this play of light and

Figure 5.2

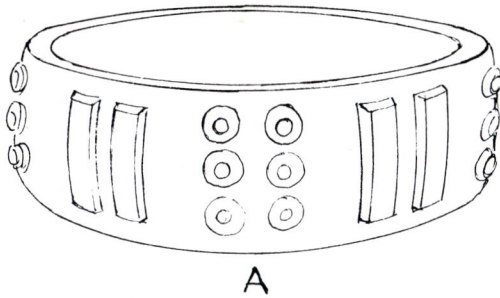

A

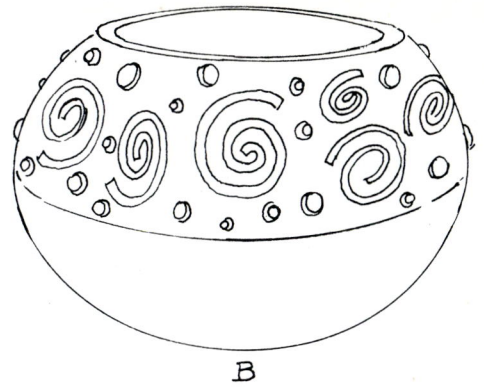

B

shadow can be most elegantly incorporated into a design. *Figure 5.3* gives some examples of carved decoration.

Carving must be carefully planned. The temptation with carving pottery is to follow the traditional patterns of wood carving and this is quite incorrect. Refer back to Chapter 2 and the discussion on the weakening of a pottery through using sharp internal corners. As most wood carving exploits sharp angles and edges, any attempt to copy wood carving panels will not only offend against the natural shape of clay bodies but will also introduce failure during firing. For the same reason serious changes in thickness of the pottery body through deeply incised lines will lead to weakness. From this it follows that a piece which is to be heavily carved must be planned for this purpose right from the beginning of the operation.

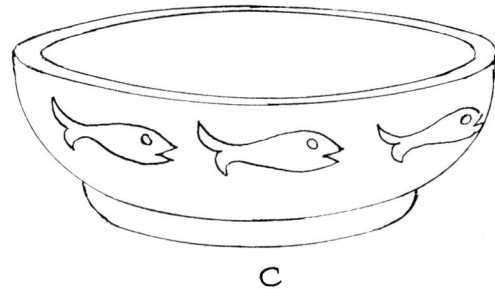

C

Pierced ware
The most elaborate of all carved decoration is to carry the carving all the way through the walls. The object so made is quite useless as a container but can have a high decorative value. It is most suited to lamp bases, particularly if a lamp is placed so as to illuminate the interior. An example of this is shown as *Figure 5.4*. On a much larger scale the technique of piercing a heavy slab can be used to make decorative screens either for screening off a portion of a room or for use outdoors. Carried to its logical conclusion, pierced ware becomes akin to ceramic sculpture.

Encaustic tiles
Inlaid tiles are the traditional type of ceramic tiles and are known as encaustic tiles. Mainly used as floor tiles the encaustic principle ensures that the pattern wears with the tile and not off it as smooth surface decorations will do. The leather hard tile is gouged out to say half the thickness of the tile and the grooves filled with a coloured clay offering a contrast to the fired clay of the body. The inserted clay must have the same shrinkage rate as the body clay and this should be tested in the way discussed in Chapter 1. The encaustic must be inserted as dry as possible and tapped firmly into place to ensure that shrinkage of this portion during drying out does not cause it to pull away from the sides of the groove. Although of greatest importance for ware subject to surface abrasion, the encaustic method can be used on most pottery and is one way to remove the disadvantage of carving a piece with too great enthusiasm, the inserted clay reinforcing the weakness from cutting too deeply.

Engobe
Slip, which is simply clay mixed with sufficient water to make a thick fluid, can be as variable as the clay from which it is made. In particular slip made from one clay can fire out a different colour to a slip or clay taken from another place. This difference in colour lends itself to the application of a coating of a coloured slip over a body of a different colour and removing part of the overlying slip to allow the contrasting colour of the body to show through in a pattern. This is the simplest, most primitive

D
applied decorations

49

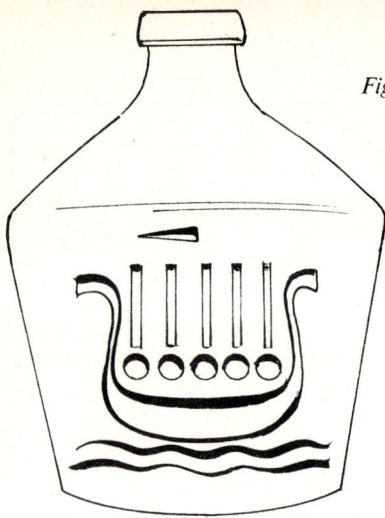
Figure 5.3

carved designs

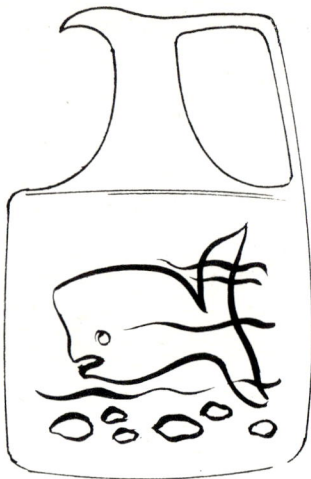
Figure 5.4

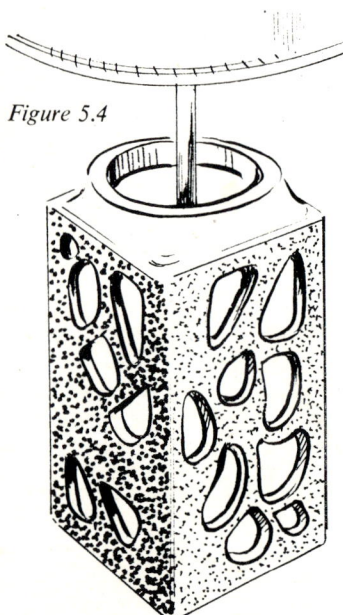
pierced ware

form of decoration possible. Slip used for the purpose of decoration is known as engobe.

Simple though the process of engobing may be, there are still a number of points which need to be known to ensure success with the operation. These are listed below for convenience of checking:

(1) The success of engobe patterns rests with the engobe staying in the right place until fused to the body during firing. To do this the engobe and the clay of the body must shrink the same amount and the only way to make sure that this is the case is to make a test piece.

(2) It greatly increases the difficulty of keeping engobe on the body if applied to a dry body. In the first place the engobe must shrink a lot further than the clay for the clay has already lost most of its water and already shrunk. Further, the dry clay will abstract water from the engobe and this extraction of water is liable to be uneven, so tending to loosen the engobe in patches. From this it follows that engobe can only be applied to reasonably moist articles and the two allowed to dry together.

(3) Possibly the simplest way to reduce difficulty with engobe is to incorporate a high percentage of body clay into the engobe and make a colour change by adding a colouring agent to this basic slip mixture. Such colouring agents are in the main metallic oxides of which more is said below under coloured engobes.

This is possibly a good a place as any to suggest that a potter can become entirely confused with the multitude of different engobes, glazes, enamels, lustres, overglazes, underglazes, and ceramic colours offered commercially to tempt him into purchasing. The only basis for selection is to first find one or two clays responsive to his particular technique. A similar number of engobes to suit the clay and a very few special glazes and other items are the only decorative requirements. All of these materials must be suited to the characteristics of the kiln to be used and the smaller the variety the higher the chance of perfecting a characteristic style.

There are many different ways to apply engobe and some of these are given consideration now.

Dipping and pouring: The simplest way to apply engobe is to mix clay well into the water and then either dip the article into the mixture or use a dipper and a draining vessel and pour the engobe over the pot. *Figure 5.5* illustrates partial dipping as a decorative technique.

Painting: Engobe is not easy to apply with a brush, it simply will not flow evenly off a brush for long brush strokes to be applied. During firing some of the engobe combines with the body of the article and delicate decorative features tend to disappear. Since long brush strokes and delicate work is non-effective, brushed patterns should be solid and able to be applied with short strokes of a heavily loaded brush .*Figure 5.6.*

Over Engobe: Using a heavy engobe, carefully poured over a thinner engobe of a contrasting or complementary colour, and trailing a tool, brush or finger through the coating, will produce some very fine decorative effects. The first engobe coating is applied by dipping, the second very

Figure 5.6

brush painting with
engobe

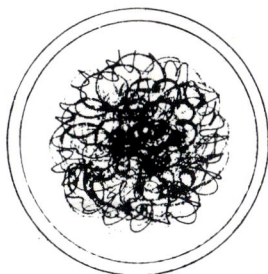

over-engobe decoration

Figure 5.5

engobe

body clay

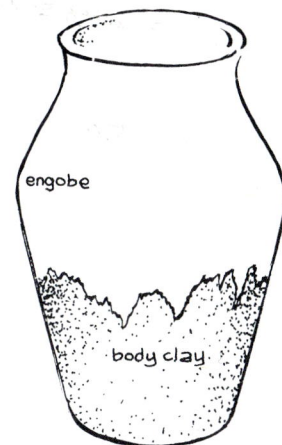

decorating by partial dipping
with engobe

carefully poured on top of the first. Use an artist's spatula or wide bladed knife almost touching the surface and pour the second coating onto the blade allowing it to flow out on to the surface. Jar the piece or swing it around to flatten the final coat. Draw the tool around and through the two coatings of engobe in almost any pattern and automatically the two engobes will tend to mix and form a fine line shaded off from the centre following the tool. *Figure 5.6.*

Engobe Trailing (Slip Trailing): Designs can be traced with engobe by trailing the material onto the piece from a tube. While special slip trailing tools can be purchased, a highly effective job can be carried out with a glass or plastic tube slightly narrowed at one end. A soda glass tube can be constricted by heating in a gas flame and pulling while soft. (*Figure 5.7*). The tube can be cut with a file at the constriction to make two slip trailers. A plastic tube can be softened in very hot water and narrowed by rolling while hot with a pencil or other round object. The trailer is filled by placing the end in the engobe and sucking up the material as if it were a soft drink being sucked through a straw. The first mouthful of clay and water will encourage caution as to how far the engobe should be drawn. Trailing engobe is regarded by many potters as the main method of applying decoration. The thickness of the pattern is regulated by the angle the trailer is held to the horizontal and a little practice will give considerable flexibility to this process.

Feathering: Very interesting effects (one example being shown in *Figure 5.8*) are given by the process of feathering, after slip trailing. In the example, heavy parallel lines of engobe were trailed across the plate and a feather drawn four times across the trails at right angles. This method can be most successful in many decorative designs. The feather is prepared by tearing away all the barbs on a fowl feather, leaving only the springy tip which is used as a drag.

Sgraffito: Sgraffito, meaning scratched, is a well known type of decoration used alone and in combination with other methods of enriching the surface of pottery. The process is simple, the design being scratched with any form of tool into the under-surface of a layer of engobe. Much variation in effect is possible. Lines scratched through wet engobe differ markedly from those scratched through dry engobe. Different tools will give different effects, combs, wire brushes, scrapers and other tools can be used as shown in the wall panel *Figure 5.9.*

Stencilling: Stencils can be cut from absorbent paper and while wet stuck to the surface of a piece. The piece is then covered with engobe and when the engobe has dried, the paper, together with the engobe upon it, carefully pulled away. Quite spectacular effects can be achieved in this way. (*Figure 5.10*).

Wax Resist: By painting the surface of a piece with molten wax, engobe patterns can be made through the failure of the engobe to stick to the waxed surface. The wax will burn off in firing. Wax resist allows of rather more delicate designs than stencils but it must not be forgotten that delicate lines can be lost in the firing of engobe.

51

Figure 5.7

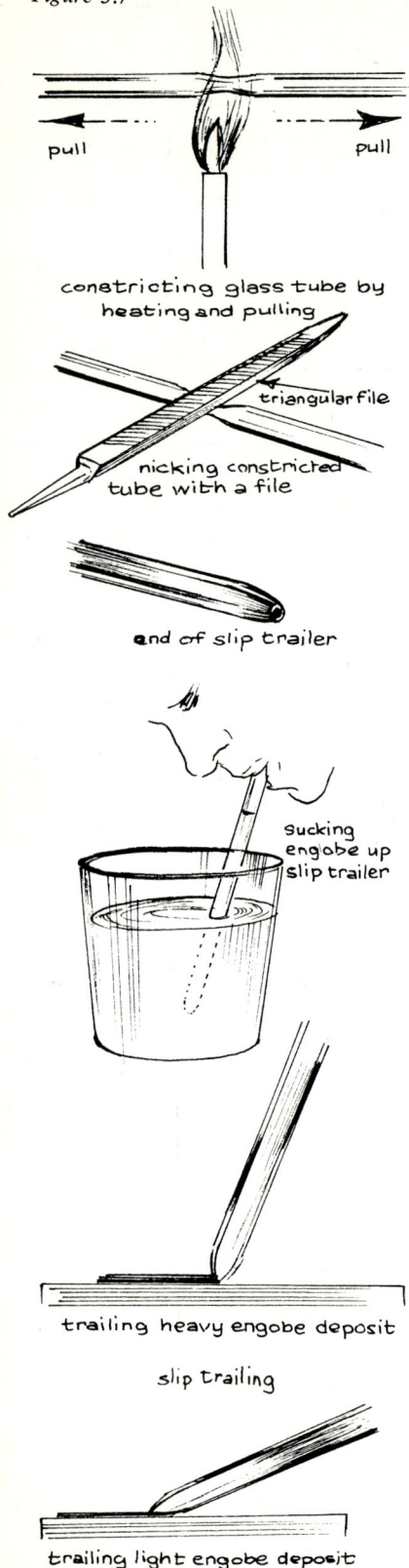

constricting glass tube by
heating and pulling

nicking constricted
tube with a file

triangular file

end of slip trailer

sucking
engobe up
slip trailer

trailing heavy engobe deposit

slip trailing

trailing light engobe deposit

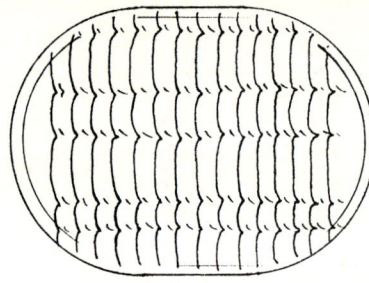

Figure 5.8

engobe feathered

Coloured engobe: The addition of coloured oxides to an engobe will give extra colour to that engobe. In theory, certain metals give certain colours but these theoretical colours are much modified by the constituents of the clay from which the engobe is made. It is easy to obtain engobing materials from commercial sources and these materials which are usually formulated to well tested recipes are more simple to use and fire truer to colour than engobes made by the potter. However, there is here, as in so many cases in dealing with pottery, reason to doubt the level of satisfaction to be gained from the unreserved use of commercial materials. If the potter is mainly interested in producing, usable, moderately attractive articles, and let us hasten to say that this is a legitimate, highly practical attitude, then it is difficult to question the use of any means which advances the ease of production. If such is the case, then proprietary brands of engobe, glaze and other decorative materials should be purchased and used as directed by the supplier. However, it is equally legitimate to doubt the amount of true creative satisfaction to be gained from the use of over-slick commercial engobes and glazes. No matter how sophisticated a studio a potter may use, as long as his pottery is dependent on being made by hand by methods which are primitive in comparison to the technological triumphs of a modern ceramic factory, then his pieces are primitive in comparison to a stamped-out, mechanically decorated, automatically fired product. This primitive, individualistic characteristic of hand-crafted pottery is the essence of the artistic creativity of good pottery. Swamping this individualism with commercial ingenuity is a loss. However, 'no man is an island' as the saying goes and just as it is impossible for a modern man to remain isolated from the technology of our society, so is it silly for a potter to attempt a dependence only on products of his own efforts. The really effective course of action is a compromise, a creative compromise that nicely balances the primitiveness of the hand thrown pot against the convenience of commercially evolved materials. All this adds up to a feeling that a slightly muddy looking finish from impurities in the clay of a coloured engobe is artistically preferable on a hand-made piece of ware than a shiny, unblemished, sparklingly clear finish from a commercial product showing up all the small defects and imperfections which are really the hallmark of hand-made ware.

If the above point of view is acceptable then a wide field of satisfaction can be gained by a potter in experimenting with colour additives in his engobes. Many will be the failures but great will be the satisfaction when there results a material which is truly his own, suited to his own requirements and stamping his ware with his creative individuality.

To begin with, three standard oxides can be used:

(1) Red Iron Oxide (Fe_2O_3): This oxide will produce a very wide range of colours somewhat variable in results owing to differences in firing. At least 5% by weight of iron oxide to the weight of dry clay should be used. A lot of experimenting is needed to obtain the best results with a given clay but some beautiful shades from amber through to tan to a deep red brown can be expected with the usual run of clay.

(2) Manganese dioxide ($Mn\ O_2$), or even better, Manganese carbonate

Figure 5.9

(Mn CO$_3$) in quantities of from 5 % to 10 % of the weight of dry clay in the engobe, can in certain circumstances fire out a glorious violet but usually in the purplish brown range.

(3) Cobalt Oxide (Co$_3$ O$_4$) or less satisfactory, Cobalt carbonate (Co CO$_3$). The strongest of all ceramic colourants, it must be used sparingly in the order of $\frac{1}{2}$ %, and produces a range of blue colours.

These three colourants will provide a wide variety of coloured engobes to be made either using them as single additives or in combination one with the other. Results can be most conveniently tested by treating small tiles made by the slab method with each sample and firing out. It is a good idea to pierce a hole in the tile when making it and note on the back details of firing, recipe used and other relevant data. These tiles can then be used as labels and tied to the neck of the storage jar in which the particular engobe is stored.

Glaze: As previously noted, engobes must be applied to green ware (ware which has not been fired and as mentioned in Chapter 6, then called biscuit or bisque ware). For many reasons it is necessary to apply decoration to ware which has been fired once and then refire it to fuse the decorative coating to the body. In other cases it is required that a coat of some protective substance be applied to give a final finish to the piece. From the plainly utilitarian point of view, glaze is in some cases essential to make pottery watertight by sealing the pores on a body which has not been heated to a temperature where the constituents of the clay have fused together. Many potters seem to believe that glazing a pot to make it watertight is the sign of a failure as a potter, true pottery being watertight on its own merits. Correct as this view may be, if the only available kiln cannot reach a high enough temperature to fuse the clay, then there is no alternative but to seal the pores with a glaze which fuses at a lower temperature And further to this question of glaze, because it will fuse, run and form a smooth surface, a glazed vessel is more easily cleaned and much more hygenic when used for food than an unglazed pot. So be it, every potter producing other than very special articles will sooner or later have need for glazes to use in his work.

Once introduced to glazes a very wide and very wondrous field is opened to a potter. Basically glazes are glass of one sort or another, using the same ingredients, more or less, as are used for glass making. Actually there can be considerable confusion in defining the difference between slip or engobe, glaze, enamel, lustre, onglaze and other terms. What one potter or pottery book calls a glaze another calls an enamel and yet another will call it a fluxed engobe. Sufficient information is given below to allow of all but specialist potters to be able to satisfy their needs.

Simple glaze

A flux is a material which among other things has the property of lowering the melting point of the constituents of normal clay. Lead is one such substance and the simplest of all glazes can be compounded to the following recipe:

Red Lead (Pb$_3$ O$_4$)	—	2 parts
Dry slip	—	3 parts

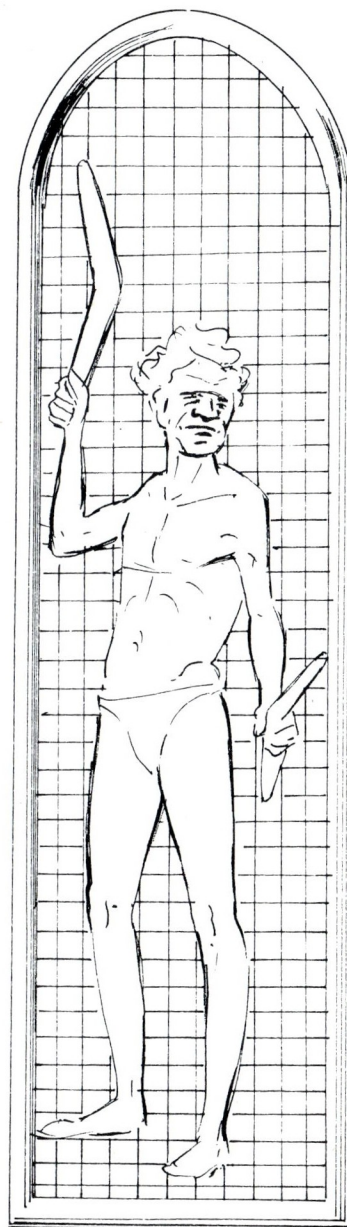

sgraffito decoration on wall panel

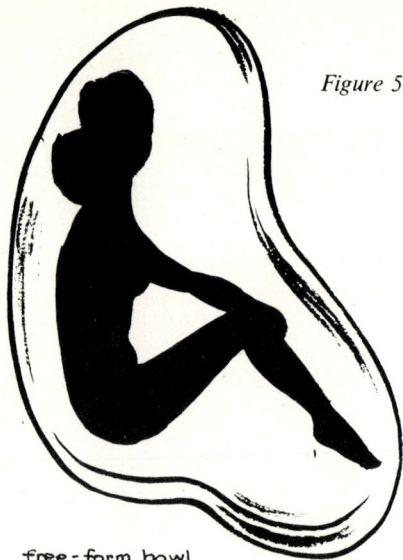

Figure 5.10

free - form bowl
- stencil decoration

This glaze is mixed with water to which has been added some epsom salts (not very much) in order to prevent the red lead from settling in a hard mass at the bottom of the container. Red lead can be readily obtained from a supplier of chemicals, is poisonous and must be treated with care. An alternative and safe glaze is made from:

Sodium silicate (waterglass) — 10 parts
Whiting   — 2 parts
Dry clay powder   — 1 part

The clay and the whiting are mixed to a thick paste with water and the waterglass is rubbed in a little at a time.

Like engobes, a glaze must fit the clay with which it is fired. Hence the above recipes are not absolute, but can be varied to suit a particular clay, fired in a particular kiln. Experiments are in order and the same experimental procedure as was suggested for engobes, should be used.

Applying glazes
Glaze is usually applied to pottery which has bisqued (see Chapter 6 for this operation). In the bisque state, pottery is porous and will absorb the water leaving a layer of glaze on the surface. If trouble is experienced with glaze flaking off before it can be fired, a small quantity of either gum arabic or preferab.y gum tregacanth (both of which can be obtained from chemical suppliers) mixed with the liquid glaze will cause it to adhere firmly to the ware.

All the methods of applying engobe can be used with glaze although it is generally recommended that most of the decoration, until such time as a potter has gained considerable experience, be done with methods other than glaze. This advice should not be interpreted as a charge that glaze decoration is difficult, for this would be untrue. It is simply that in very general terms, glaze decorations are more sophisticated in choice than other methods discussed in this chapter and until sufficient experience has been gained of simpler methods, it is not wise to over-extend one's operations.

Purchasing glazes
Most pottery suppliers offer a mystifying range of decorative mediums. The simplest solution to making a choice is to give as many particulars of one's needs, in writing, to the supplier, seek his advice and abide by his instructions.

Oxide undercolours
Unexperienced potters looking through the list of colour mediums offered by a supplier may be tempted to add colour to his ware by trying out some of the offerings. There is no reason why this should not be done but some equally colourful effects can often be obtained and at a very much lower cost by applying metallic oxides (discussed under engobes above) before the glaze is applied. These oxides can be mixed with water to which a little gum has been added to form a mixture about the consistency of thin

Figure 5.11

cream. This mixture can be applied in any of the ways mentioned under engobes above.

Defects in glazes

One eminent potter is fond of saying 'There's always an element of uncertainty in firing glazes'. A lot of his fellow potters feel that this is the understatement of the pottery world. Hope for the best and be resigned to the worst, with most results falling between the two extremes, is the experience of most potters at some stage in their career. However it is not really as bad as it seems for many faults are fairly readily identified by the result and the cause can be eliminated in future firing. For this reason a brief list of defects which commonly plague potters is given to finish this chapter, but given in the hope that no reader will anticipate that all or, for that matter, many of the faults listed will apply to his pottery.

Crazing: The development of tiny cracks over a substantial portion of the glaze. The usual cause is a poor fit between body and glaze. The remedy is to change the glaze recipe and experiment further.

Crawling: When the glaze runs and leaves bare patches. There are a number of possible causes, listed below; the remedies obviously follow from the causes.

(i) Not enough gum to hold the glaze in place.

(ii) Dust, oil, wax or dirt on the body when glazed.

(iii) Too heavy an application or too thick a flux.

(iv) Not a high enough firing temperature.

(v) Firing before the glaze dried thoroughly (a common fault through natural impatience).

Blistering: Self-evident. May be due to sulphur in the clay. Can be remedied by adding 2% of Barium carbonate to the clay when in slip form. Can often be remedied by refiring. If a persistent fault, either use a different body clay, a different glaze, (preferably one without manganese which is subject to blistering), or use a different method of decoration. May be a kiln fault, with other than electric kilns. Check air inlets and burners to make sure that sufficient oxygen is there to completely consume the fuel before reaching the firing chamber.

Pin Holes: Again self-evident, but a most annoying defect. May be caused by poorly prepared clay, too rapid firing or cooling.

Running: Self-evident. Too heavy a coating of glaze. Can also be too much flux in the glaze.

Roughness: Not enough glaze or too little flux in the glaze.

Shivering and Dunting: When either part of the glaze lifts or a section comes out of the surface of the piece. Usually owing to too rapid cooling or poorly mixed body clay. Rarely from too rapid firing.

And after the above daunting list of things that can go wrong, it may be as well to say that despite all the things that may prevent a piece of clay from finally appearing as an art form to delight the eye and give joy to the creator, many, many lumps of clay do end up as a delight to the eye.

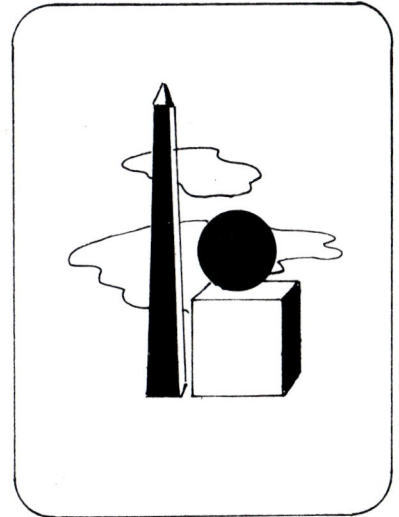

wax resist decoration on tile

CHAPTER SIX

Clay modelling techniques

Of all the clay crafts, the art of ceramic sculpture or modelling will give the greatest freedom of expression. In using the great plasticity of the original clay, artistic inspiration can be brought to fruition more quickly than with any other medium. While few ceramic pieces rank among the great masterpieces of sculpture. it is almost certain that clay has in some way played its part in the production of any sculpture. A clay model is quite often used as a master form, from which a bronze casting is finally produced. Many sculptors admit the inspiration they have at one time or another gained from experimenting with the natural forms, the fluid lines into which clay will normally develop. Unquestionably, fully plastic clay is the prime example of a natural modelling material. Indeed, man-made modelling materials are either clay to which has been added a non-drying oil so that the plasticity is permanently maintained, or a combination of waxes or other materials specifically developed to duplicate the characteristics of natural clay.

It may therefore seem strange that with the intimate connection which has always been present between clay and the major art of sculpture, that many more pieces of ceramic sculpture are not listed as masterpieces. As with all artistic creativity, this gulf between potentiality and actuality is complex but one very good reason lies in the structural limitations imposed on clay, particularly during firing. Of this, more is said below. First let us give consideration to clay as a modelling material.

Clay as a teaching aid
Freedom of form, the development of self-expression, the extraction of the natural characteristics of the material with which one is working are the essential fundamentals of artistic endeavours.

To communicate, to give expression to one's aims, one's inspirations one's aspirations, one's prime reason for being, is the ultimate of artistic creativity for which the artist continually strives.

But artistry cannot thrive, indeed cannot exist in a vacuum. Art is a two-way process. 'Neither a borrower nor a lender be' may be excellent advice in the material world, but the essence of art requires that the whole of society be both givers and receivers. The artist must give. The viewer must receive. Ideally, giver and receiver should live within each of us and particularly in the present age (and of increasing importance in the years to come) it is necessary for all of us to become both givers and receivers of that which we know of art. This driving social need is surely the reason for the community, through our schools, accepting the responsibility of encouraging the young of our society to become part of this process.

The appreciation of great art becomes easier, the more we realise our own potentiality in the field of creativity. It is in the ease of experimenting, the freedom of movement, the very fluidity of the medium that makes clay the almost perfect vehicle for the cultivation of form, design and texture as a means of expression. The only charge that can be laid against clay is that it is messy. But it is a clean mess, easily washed from hands, tables and floors and needing only the provision of simple protective clothing to adequately guard against soiled clothes.

Modelling in natural clay has the ultimate advantage over nearly all other simple modelling materials in that it can be fired to make permanent pieces which have turned out well. Such pieces can be further developed by the use of colour and second firing to introduce this further dimension in the teaching of art appreciation through taking part in artistic creativity.

Clay for modelling
The most obvious advantage of clay as an experimental art medium is its cheapness. The need to husband supplies does not exist and the lavishness of the medium used encourages an artistic freedom which can otherwise be inhibited by economy. If the simple instructions given in Chapter 1 are followed, every teacher, student, parent and child can have a plentiful supply of well-prepared clay. For modelling purposes a shorter clay containing less water and rather more sand or grog than as used in other clay crafts, is both cleaner to use and rather better for holding delicate detail. An ideal modeling clay will have the following characteristics:

(i) Be sufficiently plastic not to crack or crumble when sheets of clay are bent or rolled to form.
(ii) Be not sticky so that one's hands get covered with a wet ooze.
(iii) Be stiff enough to hold shape.
(iv) Have sufficient mutability to be changed by squeezing or other hand techniques, yet retain its new form without cracking or crumbling.

Figure 6.1

self supported ceramic figures.
The Maori hero Tane pushing Rangi,
the shy father away from Papa, the
earth mother.

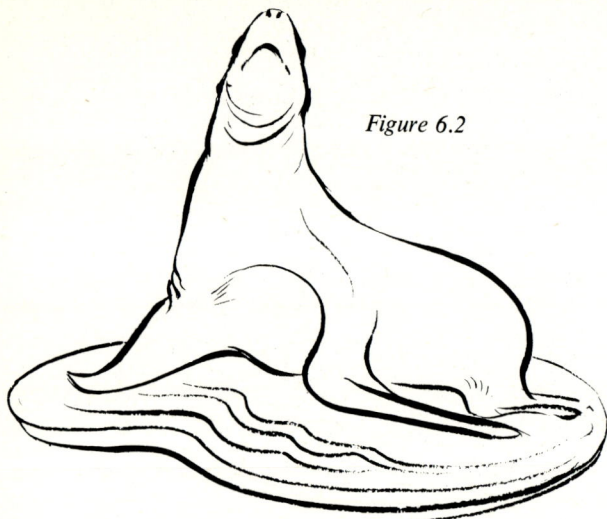

Figure 6.2

simplicity of form

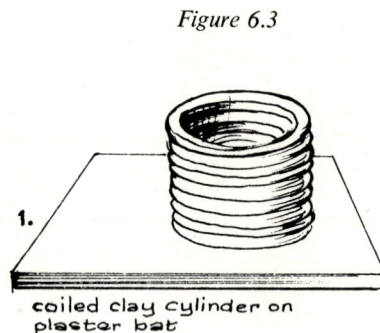

Figure 6.3

1.

coiled clay cylinder on
plaster bat

To some extent the above requirements appear to be mutually exclusive and do show that the clay needs to be well prepared and once brought to the right condition, maintained in that state, preferably in a wet box as described in Appendix B. The same piece of clay cannot be used over and over, indefinitely. From time to time, the more often the better, it should be rewedged and, to rid it of dirt and other extraneous matter, the clay should now and again be thoroughly mixed with water and treated again as slip. With the use of a little time and effort, ample supplies of clay can always be to hand for instruction and at virtually no cost.

Firing clay sculpture
Throughout this book emphasis has been placed on continued observence of the limitations of clay as a structural material. This is essential, particularly so as to avoid failure during firing. In making ceramic sculpture there is a great temptation to add a little more, balance the design by making the walls thicker, produce an unsupported piece a little further and so on. Such a state of mind will not allow success. Unkind though it may be, artistic freedom must be tempered to fit the practical needs and, for this reason, there is listed below a summary of the limits within which all fired clay structures must remain:

(1) Sharp angles, particularly internal angles will show up as a source of weakness, possibly leading to failure during firing but always remaining a place where a crack or fracture can occur.
(2) Sections of green (not fully dried out) clay can be successfully joined when in approximately the same state of dryness. Any large difference in the moisture content will result in each section shrinking at a different rate and will greatly increase the chance of failure.
(3) The shorter the clay used (as when large quantities of grog are incorporated) the less the amount of shrinkage that will take place while drying and the less the distortion during firing. So for sculpturing, clay should contain the maximum amount of grog, bringing it as close to the limits of essential plasticity as is practical.
(4) Even with clay carrying the maximum amount of grog, there is a limit to the thickness of a piece which can be successfully fired. The absolute upper limit of thickness can only be determined by trial and error for each particular clay, but every opportunity must be taken to leave hollow any part which must give the appearance of thickness. This is a most important point. It is so easy to add a little more clay here and there to achieve balance and end up with a piece almost certain to explode in the firing.

60

2. cylinder extended to lower forehead level

3. features added, modelling both from inside and out

4. top of head built up by coils

5. hollow base built up from coils

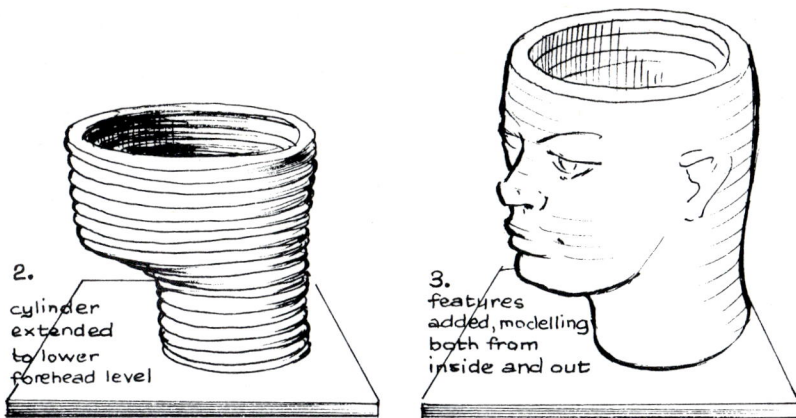

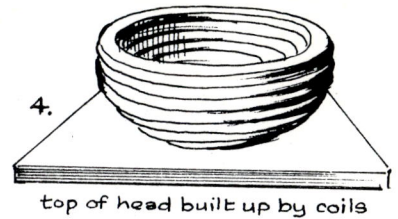

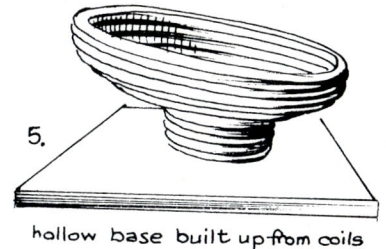

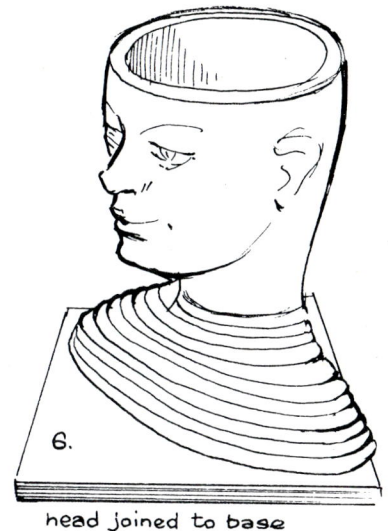

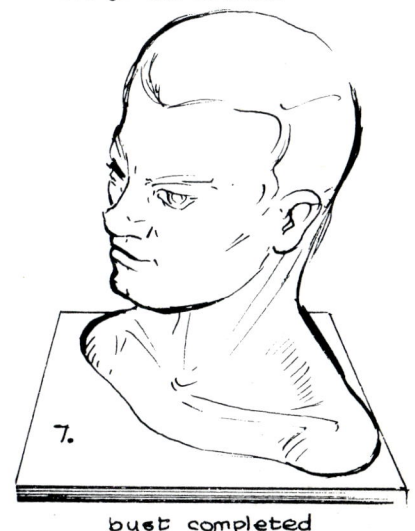

The only way to guard against such failures is to keep a determination to scrap a piece that is not going well and start again.

(5) Wet clay has a very limited amount of strength and an impatient modeller can find that a partly or wholly finished piece will slump and lose its lines through this. For this reason some sculptors find it best to simultaneously work on several pieces so allowing time for the individual pieces to gain strength through partial drying while work is being done on other pieces.

(6) Even after firing, ceramic ware is subject to damage from shock and other causes. Unsupported extensions, such as arms, legs, even the head of a piece are particularly weak points and either such extensions must be avoided in the design or where included, given extra support from other structures. This point is illustrated in *Figure 6.1*. In the ceramic sculpture piece the design has been deliberately chosen to ensure that all parts interlock and are supported.

Clay modelling techniques

All the methods of handling clay as discussed in previous chapters of this book can be used as a means of shaping clay into sculptured pieces. These various methods are again briefly discussed below with special emphasis given to modelling techniques.

Squeezed and pulled clay methods as mentioned in Chapter 3 are a logical way to produce small clay figures and pieces. These ways of working clay do lend themselves to free form development and self-expression and can be recommended for beginners, particularly children. It will be found that the thickness of a piece can often be kept within limits and the whole design lightened by carving away portions of the piece. Encouragement should be given to absolute simplicity in the design. Lack of size can be compensated for by boldness and cleanness of design. Above all balance, that indefinable something that makes a piece look right, should be the aim. Simplicity of form is illustrated in the forms shown in *Figure 6.2*.

Coil modelling: The production of pots from coils as described in Chapter 2 can be extended to sculpture. The basic shape is produced by the coil technique and the sculptured details added. This is possibly the most versatile means of producing a very wide range of shapes incorporating a hollow centre. Coil modelling lends itself well to the larger sized objects, but does require careful planning. As successful sculptors sooner or later want to try their skill on the making of a bust of the human head, one way of handling such a project is shown in some detail in *Figure 6.3*. and described below:

6. head joined to base

7. bust completed

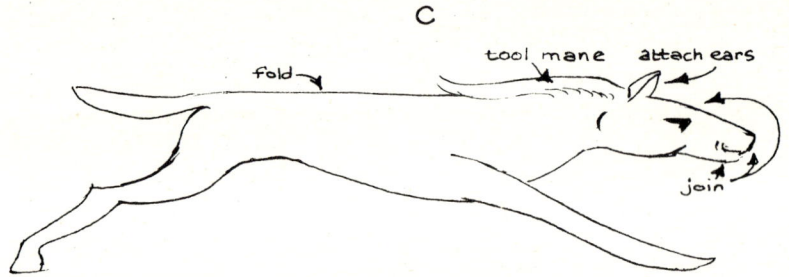

C

fold

tool mane   attach ears

join

Figure 6.4

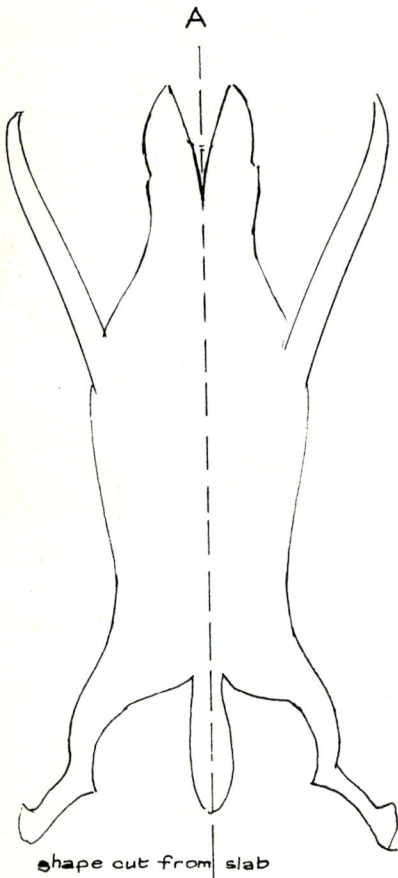

A

shape cut from slab

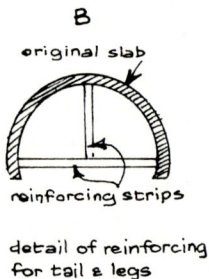

B

original slab

reinforcing strips

detail of reinforcing
for tail & legs

Step 1

A short cylinder of coiled clay is laid down on a plaster bat and put aside to gain strength by loss of moisture, after the coils have been consolidated and smoothed.

Step 2

The top coil of the base cylinder is well dampened and further coils are added, somewhat off centre as the head is developed until a position somewhere about eventual eye level is reached.

Step 3

Using both hands, one supporting the wall inside and the other pushing, modelling and moulding, bring the head to shape and apply the gross features. Care must be taken at this stage to ensure the walls are not unduly thickened at any point.

Step 4

Using the same method of coil building, make the top section of the head. Use calipers to gauge the matching size of the two sections as described in the section on two-part pots in Chapter 3.

Step 5

Build a base by coiling, this time callipering the bottom of the original cylinder to obtain the diameter of the first coil. The base should be produced somewhat beyond the desired height and the top (which will be eventually the bottom) cut level with a needle or wire. Gauge the height of the cut from the surface of the bat on which the building is being done, and mark the position of the cut at short intervals as a guide to having a level base.

Step 6

Join the base and the head similarly to the procedure adopted in Step 2.

Step 7

Finally join the top of the head to the rest of the bust and place the completed job in the wet box to condition the clay in order that the final delicate details can be tooled into the surface. A description of modelling tools is given at the end of this chapter.

Heads make fascinating pieces of sculpture and many potters find, somewhat to their surprise, a flair for capturing the likeness of their subjects. Some experience is needed to make allowance for the distortion which will inevitably take place in the alignment of the features as the clay dries out, but this is usually not too serious and can be overcome with a little practice. It may be mentioned that a potter who can produce a reasonable ceramic portraiture of subjects will have small difficulty in obtaining lucrative commissions as a reward for his skill. The same procedure as outlined above can obviously be used for many pieces other than busts.

Slab modelling

This may be used much in the same way as the coil method above for producing the basic shape for further working (as can in some cases throwing) and the various methods of moulding as described in Chapter 4. However, the slab method of handling clay lends itself admirably to the production of folded shapes in three dimensions so suited to modern modes. This method of production is shown in *Figure 6.4* and described below. It is particularly suited to the making of stylised animal forms.

(1) A pattern is drafted first one side only, the paper folded along the line of the back and the other identical side traced through the paper using a fine blunt tool to impress through both thicknesses of paper.

(2) The pattern is laid on a prepared slab of clay and the fine tool used to impress the pattern onto the slab surface.

(3) Use a needle and cut the shape vertically to the surface – *Figure 6.4A*.

(4) Drape the shape over a round support; a piece of wooden dowelling will do for this *Figure 6.4B*.

(5) Join the section down the face but usually nowhere else.

(6) Shape the legs, the tail and any other appendages to a convex structurally strong shape and if the piece is large, add reinforcing strips of slab clay as shown in *Figure 6.4C*.

(7) Finish by attaching any minor items separately, for instance the ears in *Figure 6.4C* and tool in eyes, mane and any other details.

The model must be supported until dry enough for the legs to support the weight. Very similar methods can be used for original designs of the type shown in *Figure 6.5*.

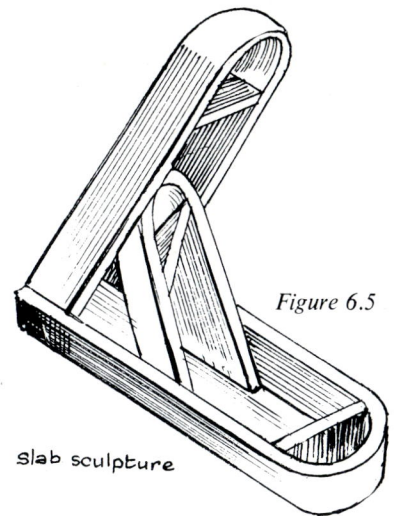

Figure 6.5

slab sculpture

Carved and incised sculpture

Bas-relief figures may be carved into clay panels. Bas-relief offers an entirely satisfying dimension in creativity. The design is carved, incised or modelled into the surface of a panel and gives an almost unlimited scope for imagination. The real difficulty is to make certain that the parts of the design raised do not produce a thickness beyond the limits of the firing of the panel. This difficulty can be completely avoided by incising the whole way through the panel design as was suggested in Chapter 5 under the heading of Incised Decoration. Where complete cut out decoration will not serve and where raised figures end up in too great a thickness of material, the only other alternative is to carve out portions of the back of the panel when the clay has dried to the leather stage. If those portions under the figures are alone carved out there is no loss of structural strength. *Figure 6.6* shows a design suited to bas-relief for a child's room.

This method of reducing the thickness of clay walls is a solution to the difficulty of firing a solid figure. Chinese craftsmen have used this solution for centuries and it answers very well where the carving can be carried out from below, as is the case with an animal for instance standing or lying horizontally. It is also a practical solution for sculptures designed to fit against a wall or in a niche or some other place where the hollowed portion of the sculpture will not be normally seen.

Figure 6.6

bas-relief

Figure 6.7

splashing plaster in splash moulding

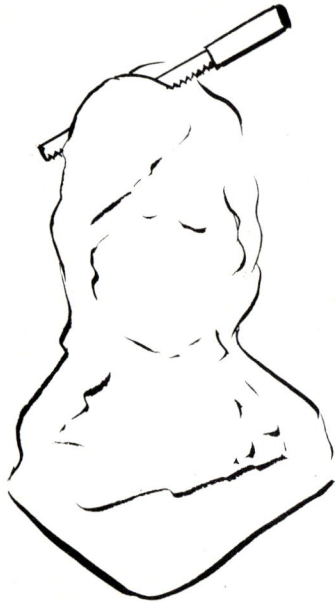

halving mould

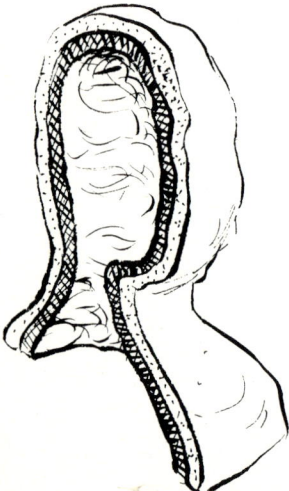

clay pressed into half mould

Moulded Sculpture

The most elaborate technique and the one that gives an answer to practically all problems of keeping the walls of sculptured pieces within firing limits, is the sculpturing of a master form, making a mould from this form and using this mould as the pattern in which the finished piece is made. This is a highly sophisticated technique and capable of yielding rich and and exciting art pieces. *Figure 6.7* shows the step by step procedure which is outlined below:

(1) A master form is sculptured from solid clay. With a large solid figure such as this the shrinkage is liable to be very great and is reduced by building up the centre of the mould with large pieces of grog. Only sufficient clay should be used to bind the grog and then a layer of plastic clay, well grogged itself, of barely sufficient depth to take all surface details is plastered on the outside.

(2) The gross details of the figure are modelled into the plastic clay and the fine details tooled in when the clay is almost at the leather stage and the figure left to dry out fully.

(3) The technique of splash moulding is used for a large piece such as is worthy of this method. The plaster is mixed to a fairly liquid consistency and then either thrown by hand or splashed onto the master form with a thin layer of plaster.

(4) As the first layer of plaster starts to set, a second layer of plaster is applied, reinforcing the plaster with strips of open-weave cloth.

(5) Successive layers of cloth and plaster are built up to a thickness of $\frac{1}{2}$ an inch or more.

(6) Carefully, with a fine tooth saw, cut the mould into two halves. The saw blade must be worked around the mould, penetrating right through the walls of the mould but not sufficiently deep to strike the grog reinforcing within the master form.

(7) At this stage the mould is in two parts which are cleared of any remains of the master form and well washed with cold water.

(8) Each half of the mould is used as a press-in mould (described in Chapter 4) and walls of clay built up to a suitable thickness inside each half, pressing and consolidating the clay firmly.

(9) Extra clay is left above the edges of each half of the mould and this is well dampened until a fully plastic state is reached. Then the two parts of the mould are pressed firmly together and held either with a series of heavy rubber bands or being tied wth tight cord.

(10) The extra clay to form the joint between the two halves will be extruded either inside the figure or on to the outside of the mould. When sufficient time has been left for the clay to fully dry, the mould is separated and the figure, now free of the plastic owing to shrinkage, removed.

(11) The joint seam can be cleaned away and the final finish given to the figure by tooling. This technique is an elegant method, capable of dealing with most intricate figures if a multipart mould is used. Where the mould

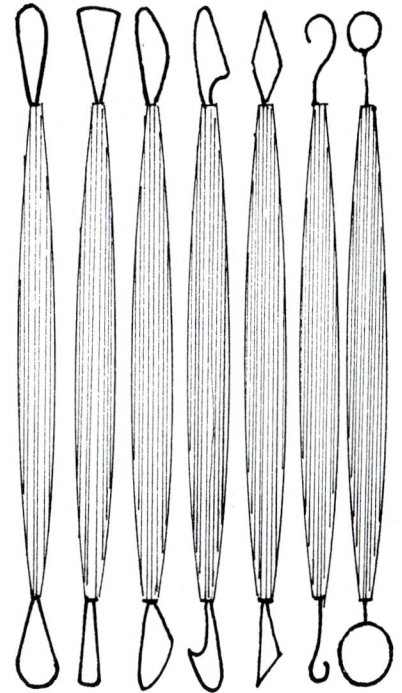

Figure 6.8

group 1.

is made of more than two parts, thin metal (shim metal is very thin and can be cut with scissors) shim strips are set on edge into the master form and the plaster thrown on either side of the metal strip which then acts as a divider for the separation of the parts of the mould.

Finishing sculptures
More than any other ceramic piece, a sculpture should be able to stand alone in the elegance of its design, form, balance and texture without recourse to elaborate decorative effects. Terra cotta is the classical unglazed finish of clay sculpture. Terra cotta, which is literally translated into 'baked earth' is the natural finish and when textured by one of the methods suggested below, has a very special appeal: some surface finishes easy to obtain include the following:

(1) Rubbing with a smooth metal tool, the rounded side of a spoon for instance will give an almost polished surface. This is the way to raise natural highlights to accent a particular feature.
(2) Use of a damp sponge will bring the grog in the clay into relief and leave a sandy finish.
(3) Pressing a coarse textured cloth lightly into the plastic surface of a figure will leave an imprint of the weave of the cloth.
(4) Tools of various sorts, combs, fingers, nail marks and anything else that will leave an impression on the surface can be appropriately used for special effects.

The one place where colour is really appropriate and a glazed finish an advantage, is for garden sculptures. For this work any of the decorative finishes discussed in Chapter 5 can be used.

Modelling tools
The number of modelling tools available for use in clay modelling is almost infinite. Every possible shape, degree of sharpness and form seems possible. A few illustrations from a supplier's catalogue are depicted in *Figure 6.8* and the appropriate catalogue descriptions are given below.

Group 1
'A precision instrument, it is a modelling and cutting tool in one. It features a double ground, knife edge of high-temper steel, for exact, detailed carving of plaster, clay and wax and fine enough to do the minutest modelling.'

'For a new creative experience for both professional and amateur – try these exceptional modelling tools once and you'll never work with another.'

One is tempted to wonder whether the double ground, knife edge will cut off all fingers to ensure that one will never work with another.

Facetiousness apart, one or two tools from this group are excellent for surface carving, hollowing figures and trimming in wheel work.

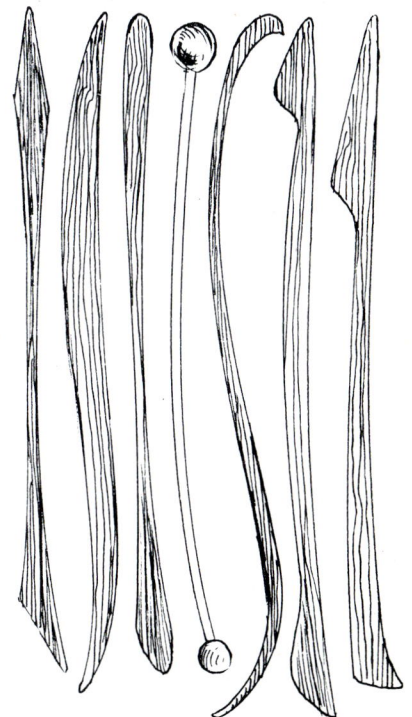

group 2.

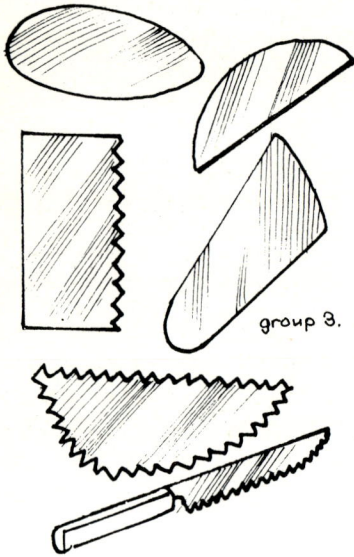
group 3.

Figure 6.8

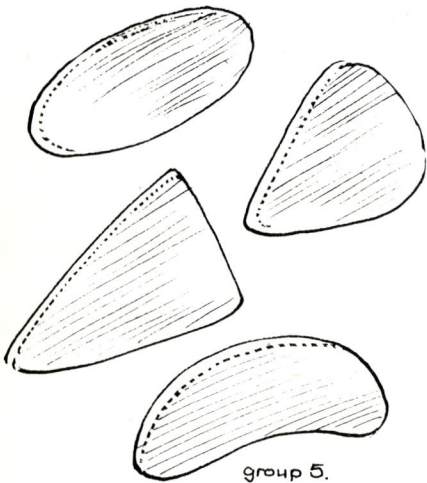
group 4.

Group 2

'A new experience in modelling, costs less than rigid, unyielding, old-fashioned, wood tools. Smooth polished surfaces model with ease on all types of clay without sticking. Modern plastic technology makes the best of all possible tools.'

Tools in this group can readily be made out of wood by the potter as the need arises. The possible exception to this is the ball ended tools of particular use in smoothing internal joints in the making of two-piece pots and similar articles where the entrance is not large enough to insert one's hand.

Group 3

'The best tools for smoothing, removing lumps and bumps, making perfect surfaces on plaster and clay forms. Toothed scrapers for textured surfaces, quick removal of unwanted material and for the quick execution of decorative effects. Made from the highest quality steel.'

Scrapers of the type of this group are most useful but once again the potter can make these for himself and they need not be made from the highest quality steel, many craftsmen manage to get by with scrapers made from a flattened tin can.

Group 4

'Turning tools for shaping clay and plaster – 9 inches long of the finest hardened steel, ground razor sharp, of rugged construction.'

These tools are of rather doubtful merit in shaping thrown pieces. They make excellent paint scrapers, but many potters who have no particular urge to scrape paint, manage to do without them.

Group 5

'Half-hard rubber palettes, ideal for finishing plastic clay.'

With this we must agree. Particularly useful in the final shaping of matching thrown pots, a semi-flexible rubber palette will give easy control of contours in the process of shaping on the wheel. The only mystery is the lack of the superlatives used in the previous exhortations to purchase. Superlatives that tend towards the belief that collecting pottery tools gives a greater creative satisfaction than using them. A belief which, if true, would make the craft superfluous and with this no potter would ever agree.

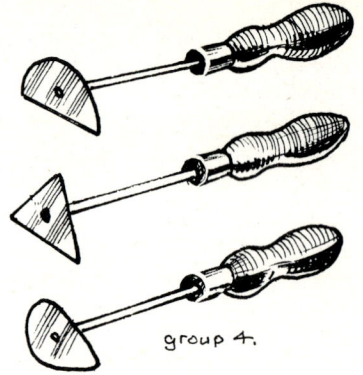
group 5.

CHAPTER SEVEN

Firing–from clay to ceramics

Pottery is not one craft, it is a number of interconnected though not necessarily related crafts. This is a part of any great craft. In pottery, a participant must grow capable in a number of techniques and perforce become a master of one or more particular facets in which there will be a tendency to specialize.

For a clay piece to become a pot or other type of pottery it must be fired. Somebody must test it by flame whether this is the creator of the piece or some outsider.

The act of firing pottery is the point of no return. All the faults, the slip-shod workmanship, the errors of commission and omission, all the impatience, come out in the firing. After firing, the piece that has been the source of inspiration or exasperation, a joy or a trial, is either a success or a complete failure. There are no half-way measures and that accounts in part for the fascination of firing clay, the proof, so to speak, of the pudding which is put within the kiln and of the somewhat unexpected results that are sometimes taken out.

Kilns and the choice of fuel
Natural Gas: Great news for the enthusiastic potter is the advent of natural gas. A far hotter fuel than manufactured coal gas, natural gas is almost certainly the best available fuel for large amateur and semi-commercial pottery kilns.

Fuel Oil: As an efficient fuel, heating oil has much to commend its use. Small drip-fed oil fired kilns relying on natural draft are practical but to obtain full efficiency an electrically operated blower fan to feed air to the kiln is necessary.

Coke fired kilns: Coke has been the main fuel of a large number of small potters for many years and will continue to so be for many years to come. It can no longer be considered as the cheap fuel it once was owing to the abandonment of many town gas manufacturing plants where coke was produced as a by-product.

Wood burning kilns: The refuge of the primitive at heart, the wood burning kiln has a special something about it that appeals to a section of the pottery community. Decidedly impractical for a commercial venture and hardly less so for the average potter, nevertheless pottery made to be fired in a wood firing kiln has an air about it that more sophisticated ware cannot match. It may be that the psychology of a potter devoted to a mode of manufacture reminiscent more of primitive times than of today brings to his ware an authenticity that makes his ware something special.

Electric kilns: Electrically heated kilns are the ultimate in convenience and mechanization. The outside dimensions of an electric kiln are small in comparison to the internal capacity; no fumes or smoke are given off and hence no flue is required; they are almost fire-proof and are easily controlled. For the casual potter living in a city with little free space, an electric kiln is the only choice. Electrically heated kilns are bought ready-made, only needing to be lifted into place and plugged into an electricity supply to be ready for use. There is, however, a serious limitation on the upper capacity of an electric kiln which can be supplied by electrical energy drawn from a domestic wiring system. A kiln large enough for a commercial operation will require new arrangements for the supply of electricity with probably new wiring being required and this in itself makes an expensive job of installing one of the larger sized electric kilns. There is also an upper limit imposed on the temperature to which an electric kiln may be safely raised. These two points should be well discussed with the supplier from whom an electric kiln may be purchased.

Types of kilns

In very general terms, kilns can be divided into three classes:

(i) Updraft in which the firing chamber is part of the flue system. The simplest type to build and the least economical in fuel. (*Figures 7.1, 7.3 and 7.4*).

(ii) Downdraft in which the complications of construction are offset by savings in fuel costs. Usually reserved for large commercial kilns. *Figure 7.2.*

(iii) Dead Air Kilns of which the electric kiln is a typical example. The flame cannot reach the ware and hence no chemical reaction can take place between the products of combustion from the burning fuel and the outside layers of the piece being fired. While this is a distinct advantage in most instances, it does tend to reduce the number of unexpected and fantastically exciting results from the chemical reactions in open flame kilns.

Muffle kilns

When it is necessary to keep the ware from the flames (as is the case with many types of glazed finishes), a flame type kiln can be fitted with a muffle. A muffle is a chamber made of highly refractory material into which is placed the ware to be fired. The flames pass around the muffle bringing it to the required temperature to fire the ware within and yet do not contact the ware. More fuel is required to reach firing temperature when a muffle is used as compared to an open firing. (See *Figure 7.1*).

Saggers

Figure 7.6 illustrates yet another practical way to keep kiln flames away from pottery ware. Clay boxes called saggers can be bought or made by the potter and when packed with ware for firing, are placed within an open flame chamber. Both a muffle and the use of saggers reduce the usable space within. (Also see *Figure 7.2*).

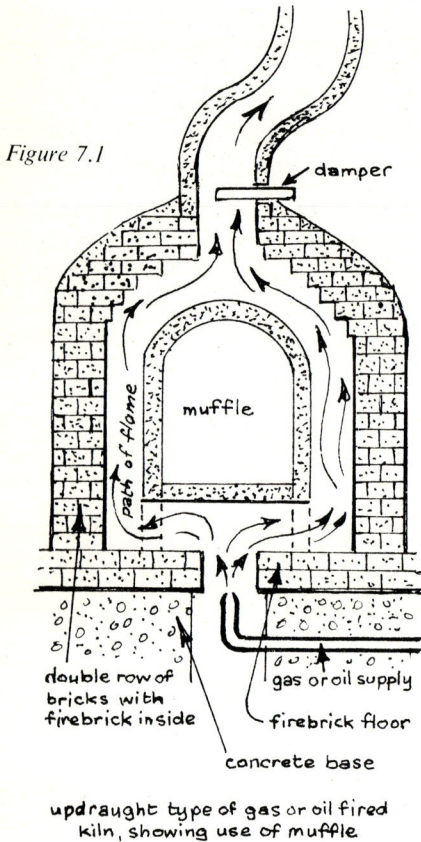

Figure 7.1

updraught type of gas or oil fired kiln, showing use of muffle

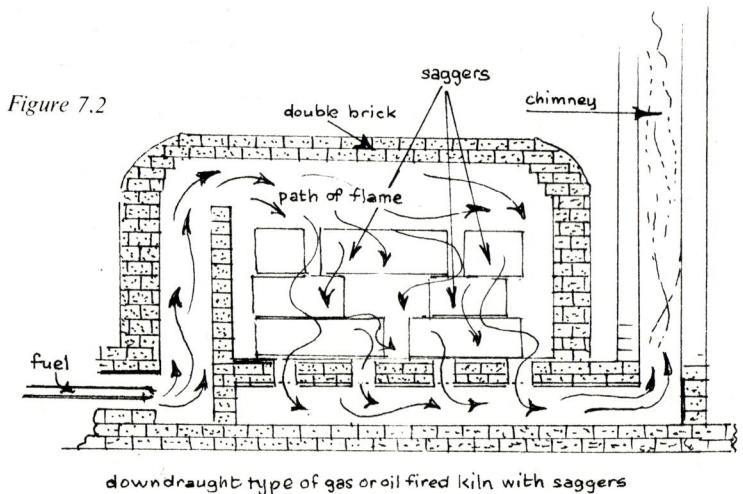

Figure 7.2

downdraught type of gas or oil fired kiln with saggers

Firing

The art of firing pottery ware can be summed up in two words – 'GO SLOWLY'. Details of a firing schedule applicable to any kiln are given below:

(i) Heat slowly, control the draft and dampers if applicable; the gas or oil tap for that type of kiln or the control of an electric kiln so that it takes 8 hours or more for the kiln to come to a temperature of 1060°C. (A temperature table follows this section.) Always follow the maker's instructions for a kiln that has been purchased ready-made and be prepared for a few failures in the beginning. Even more failures can be expected until experience is gained with a home-built kiln.

(ii) During the first part of the firing, the atmospheric water is driven from the piece. This is the 'water smoking' period of the potter. It is during this time that raw pieces which have not been fully dried will 'blow up'. To be safe, allow extra time for clay pieces to dry fully. Hold the piece against the cheek. If it feels in the slightest bit damp, dry it out some more. Take it slowly, extra slowly at this stage.

(iii) As the temperature rises, organic material in the clay breaks down. This is especially true of the red/brown clays which owe a lot of their raw colour to organic acids. Such clays can split at the above temperature and it is still necessary to be patient in allowing the kiln to come slowly up to heat.

(iv) The kiln interior then begins to show red hot. It is around about this temperature that a physical change takes place in the silica which is a constituent of all clays. This physical change involves an increase in the size of the material as the temperature rises, so stressing the structure while this expansion takes place. This is a critical point in both the heating and cooling of the kiln. The normal signs of too fast a rate of either heating or cooling through the silica change point, are cracks penetrating into the body of the piece. If the edges of such cracks are rounded, giving indications of the sharp corners having flowed, it shows that it was on the upward rise of the temperature that the damage was done. Conversely, sharp-edged cracks give notice that the cooling rate was too rapid.

(v) As the interior of the kiln shows a bright cherry red it is a sign that the worst is past or at any rate any damage which has not already been done will not be so likely to occur until the heat is turned off. The rate of heating can now be increased. The interior of the kiln will turn orange and begin to fade off to a yellow. Most clays will have matured at this stage and the heating can cease.

(vi) Now begins the long period of waiting. The kiln must cool even more slowly than it heated. Beware of draughts! Open the door on a hot kiln and there can be heard fascinating musical pings and chimes as cherished pieces fall to pieces through unequal cooling. Large kilns will require at least 24 hours to cool. Smaller kilns less time, but not much less. This is the reason why successful potters have iron-bound wills and usually fingers gnawed nearly to the wrist.

The above is the barest outline of firing procedures. Every kiln, every clay and every glaze formula requires a different firing and cooling cycle which the individual potter must learn for himself. Anticipate failures until experience is gained, for failures are the normal thing when learning to operate with new materials and especially with an unknown kiln. Never lose patience and never despair for these two attributes mark the true potter.

Kinds of pottery

Pottery is loosely referred under a number of headings. Earthenware, Stoneware, China, Porcelain, are four common ones and the way these terms are applied can be very confusing. We cannot hope to define these accurately but below we make an attempt to show some distinction between each of the above four:

Figure 7.3

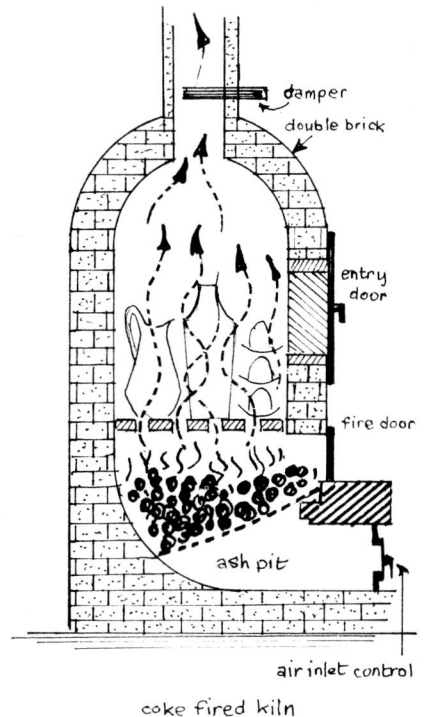

coke fired kiln

71

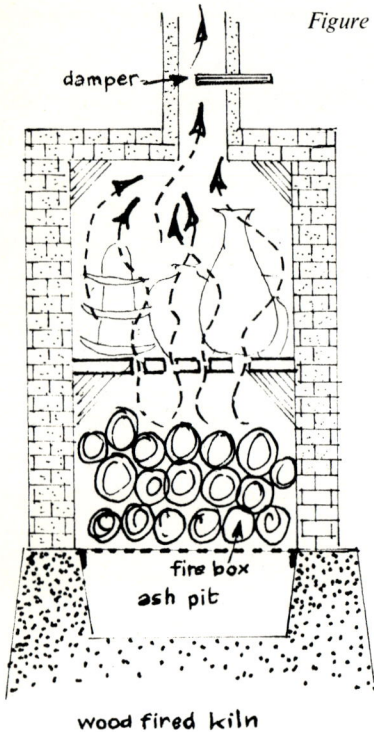

Figure 7.4

damper

fire box
ash pit

wood fired kiln

(1) Earthenware – the type of pottery which will, in general, result from following the discussion in this book. Made from natural clay without the addition of other agents, earthenware is 'fired out' to maturity at a temperature lying between 950°C and 1165°C. Again in fairly broad terms, earthenware fired at the above temperatures will be 'non-vitreous' in that it is comparatively soft, somewhat porous and will not hold liquid unless given a coating of glaze. In body colour, earthenware is often buff, red or some quite dark shade.

(2) Stoneware – very often made from natural clay alone; stoneware can be made from what are referred to as 'prepared clay bodies' which are a mixture of natural clays and additives such as flint, fire clay and other materials which reduce the plasticity of the body of the piece at a high temperature. Stoneware is fired to a temperature up to 1260°C to 1300°C which is far too high a temperature for electric kilns not fitted specially to reach this temperature. Not all clays can stand these high temperatures. Many red clays for instance will melt into a puddle on the bottom of the kiln at less than 1200°C. Finished stoneware is hard, fully vitreous so that it will ring like a piece of crystal when struck and fully waterproof without glazing. Stoneware has many advantages over earthenware and most potters wish to graduate to this class of ware sooner or later. What is not always remembered is that stoneware is subject to limitations as well as advantages and these limitations are not wholly confined to the techniques of production. Certainly this is only an opinion, but some potters who have experienced the making of stoneware have returned to the lesser difficulties of earthenware production as offering more scope and width of creativity. This is a point of view that should be studied before any potter hastens into the field of stoneware production.

(3) China – is never made from natural clay alone. It is produced in two or more firings, the first one at a high temperature in excess of 1300°C. A temperature where the interior of the kiln becomes incandescently white and ordinary fire bricks have a limited life. The second firing is to about 1160°C for fluxing. China as a term is the loosest of the four under discussion, but in general Kaolin or China clay forms a high percentage of the body and the usual colour of the body is white. Special kilns are required for firing china and there are few amateurs or semi- professional potters who have the equipment to produce china.

(4) The line drawn between what is china and what is porcelain is very ill-defined. Generally, porcelain is a purer form of china body raised to a vitrifying temperature. Porcelain is very often finished in the one firing at a really vicious temperature close to 1400°C, the body and glaze fusing into one vitrified whole. The very high temperature results in extreme hardness and greater resistance to thermal shock than that possessed by any other pottery. Thermal shock is caused by sudden changes in temperature stressing the ware beyond its fracture point and porcelain is much less liable to breakage from the cause than china as the next in the scale. Because of the high density and great strength imparted by the extreme temperature, porcelain can be made lighter and thinner, without loss of

strength, than can other pottery ware. Porcelain making is well beyond the reach of the average pottery kiln which would itself melt before porcelain vitrifying temperatures were reached.

Temperature checks
The temperature to which the kiln is raised is important. There are a number of ways of doing this as discussed below:

(1) The really primitive potter has success judging the temperature of his kiln simply by glancing through a peep-hole and assessing the colour of the kiln interior. This facility in judgement is much to be envied and bespeaks long years of experience. The less primitive potter augments his experience by the use of test slips, a procedure which can be followed at minimum expense by all.

(2) A test slip as seen by *Figure 7.7* consists of a small strip of clay with one end raised and pierced with a hole in which engages a test prod to hook the slip from the kiln. About four or six test slips are made from the actual clay in use. They are completely dried out and loaded into the kiln with the ware to be fired. Placing the test slips in a position convenient to the peep-hole in the kiln allows a slender hooked metal rod to be inserted into the kiln and a test slip to be extracted from time to time. In this way way progress within the kiln can be watched in the most practical way possible. When a slip is extracted which rings when tapped, the kiln has reached the required temperature.

Pyrometric Cones
Seger or pyrometric cones are little pyramids made of clay to which the correct quantity of a material known as a flux has been added so that the pyramids will melt at known temperatures. A number, indicating the temperature at which the cone will melt and bend is stamped on the side of the cone. By setting a number of cones, each with a different melting point into a lump of clay (known as a 'cone pat'), and placing this series inside the kiln, the actual temperature within the kiln can be discovered by noting which cones have bent and which are still standing. Hence the kiln, as at that time, has reached a temperature higher than the rating of the bent cone but lower than the temperature of the standing cone. (*Figure 7.8* shows the operation of pyrometric cones and the table at the end of this section gives the temperature code of the cones).

Pyrometers
More sophisticated than the other two temperature indicators is the electrically operated pyrometer, a dial type instrument, giving a continuous reading of the temperature within the kiln. The pyrometer operates on the electrical voltage which can be produced in certain apparatus when held at an elevated temperature, a voltmeter which records this voltage being directly calibrated to read temperature. A most convenient instrument in use, the electrical pyrometer has in late years been developed to be highly reliable in operation and reasonably economical to purchase. It

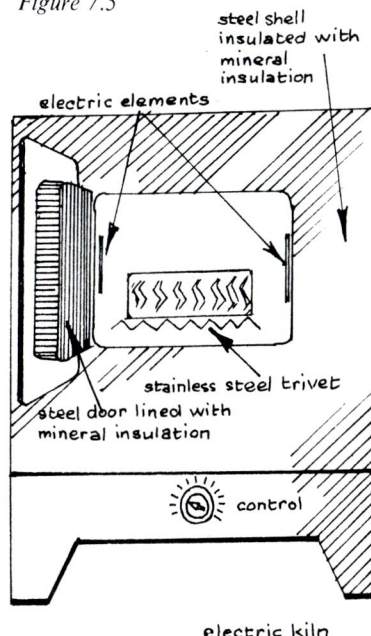

Figure 7.5

electric kiln

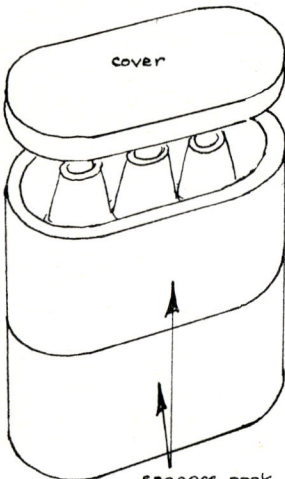

cover

saggers pack
one above the other in the
kiln, each sagger acting
as a lid for the one
immediately below.

saggers

should be noted that an ordinary thermometer is entirely useless for taking the temperature of a pottery kiln, the operating temperatures being far beyond the range of such instruments.

Optical pyrometers – At very high temperatures, such as used in porcelain firing, the electrical pyrometer suffers some limitations, the most serious of which being the melting of the sensing element. At these temperatures the optical pyrometer is essential and it is the most elegant of temperature sensors at lower temperatures as well. Optical pyrometers to do an effective job are expensive and hardly warranted for an average pottery studio. In operation the optical pyrometer compares the colour within the kiln against the colour of the filament of a small lamp within the instrument. The lamp filament and hence the colour, can be varied by the operator and this variation is graduated and very accurately indicates the temperature within the kiln. The great advantage of instruments such as this is the absence of any physical connection between the pyrometer and the kiln, the colour of the light from within the kiln being the basis of the temperature judgement.

Kiln Temperature Guide

Cone No.	Centi- grade	Fahren- heit	Colour	What Happens
022	605	1121	—	Water smoke.
018	720	1328	Dull Red	Water smoke.
014	830	1526	Red	Organic matter burnt out. Silica change begins.
012	875	1607	Cherry Red	Glazes Mature.
09	930	1706	Orange	Low fire earthenware matures.
06	1015	1859	Bright Orange	Red Clay matures.
03	1115	2039	Deep Yellow	Buff Clay matures.
01	1145	2093	Bright Yellow	All earthenware matured.
4	1190	2174	Light Yellow	Red Clay melts.
8	1260	2300	White	Stoneware matures.
13	1350	2462	Incandescent White	Porcelain matures.

While the temperatures given above are accurate, the colour is an indication only. While the last column gives an indication of what happens with typical clays, large departures from the above typical reactions can and do occur with individual clays. The action of a particular clay can only be accurately known by a procedure of trial and error.

Stacking the kiln

Most books on pottery go to great lengths to explain the proper procedure for packing a kiln. Undoubtedly space is at a premium within a pottery kiln but it does seem strange, assuming that a craftsman who can find his way through a complicated craft, lacks the ability to sensibly load a kiln. There are only a few not completely obvious points to note, such as:

(1) Above a red heat, earthenware will be sufficiently soft to warp if supported unequally.

(2) Glaze will run quite surprising distances when hot and may stick pieces together if there is any path at all down which it may travel.

(3) Kiln furniture (of which more is said under), together with the kiln interior, can be protected from glaze by painting with –

    Powdered flint – 1 part ⎱ Obtainable at Pottery
    China clay   – 1 part ⎰   Suppliers.
    Mix with water to the consistency of thick cream.

(4) High glaze finishes can be ruined with minute particles of kiln dirt. Blow out with a reversed vacuum cleaner from time to time.

(5) Find your own way of stacking and firing.

Kiln furniture

There is a wide range of commercial furniture available to act as shelves and supports in allowing more ware to be packed into the kiln than otherwise would be the case. Similarly, there are ceramic and stainless steel pieces designed to prevent glazed pottery from touching. All these extras do have their uses, but can hardly be regarded as essential. As with so much else in pottery, it is probably wise to wait until the need arises before outlaying money on apparatus not likely to pay for itself.

And that brings to a close all that can be said here on the very big question of firing pottery. At the best, firing pottery is a delightful experience, providing the first thrill of seeing a 'thing' of real beauty emerging from the flames (so to speak). At its worst, firing pottery can be a thorously frustrating business, making the most amiable of craftsmen act somewhat less than human. It is always an exercise in patience and perseverence and it can with truth be said that in the ultimate there is far more joy than sorrow, continually coming from the kilns of the fraternity of potters.

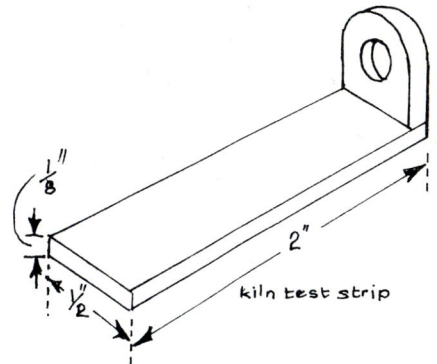

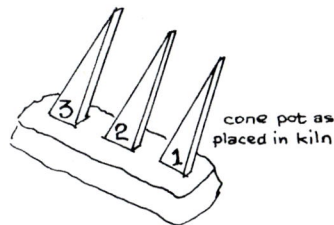

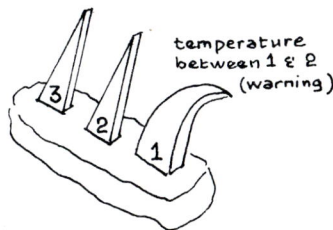

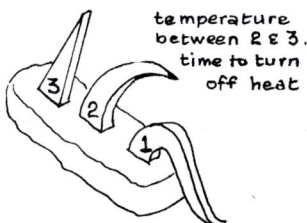

kiln test strip

cone pot as placed in kiln

temperature between 1 & 2 (warning)

temperature between 2 & 3. time to turn off heat

Appendices

APPENDIX A. The making of plaster bats.
Take a basin, preferably a soft plastic (PVC) vessel and half fill with water. Sprinkle plaster of Paris onto the water & let sink. When enough has been added so the plaster reaches the surface (having 'taken up' water in the process), stir briskly and pour into mould.

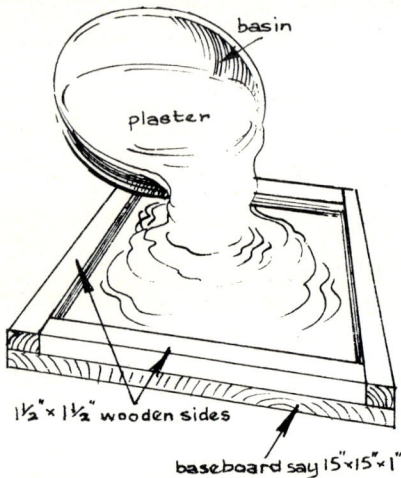

basin

plaster

1½" × 1½" wooden sides

baseboard say 15"×15"×1"

Filled to the top the above mould will make 12"×12"×1½" plaster of Paris slabs.

APPENDIX B

Construction details of 'damp box'

rubber band to close bag

loose plastic bag completely surrounding box

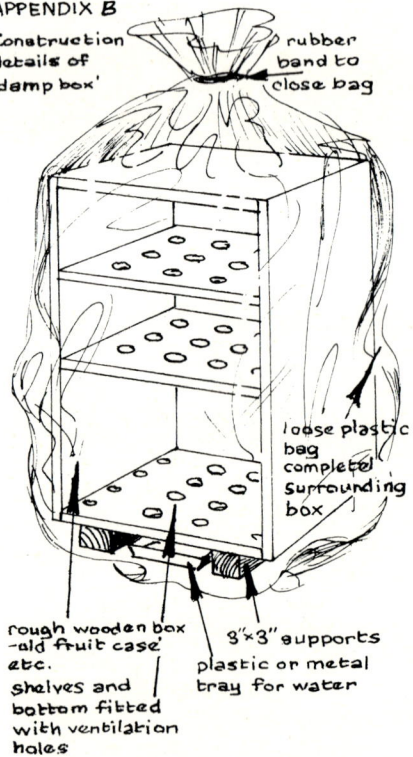

rough wooden box –'old fruit case' etc.
shelves and bottom fitted with ventilation holes

3"×3" supports
plastic or metal tray for water

adjust amount of water in tray to give correct degree of humidity inside damp box